The Humor and Drama of Early Texas

George U. Hubbard

Republic of Texas Press
Plano, Texas

Library of Congress Cataloging-in-Publication Data

Hubbard, George U.
   The humor and drama of early Texas / George U. Hubbard.
       p.   cm.
   Includes bibliographical references and index.
   ISBN 1-55622-843-0
   1. Texas—History—Humor.   2. Texas—History—Anecdotes.   I. Title.

   F386.6 .H84 2002
   976.4—dc21   2002010240

Republic of Texas Press is an imprint of Wordware Publishing, Inc.
No part of this book may be reproduced in any form or by
any means without permission in writing from
Wordware Publishing, Inc.

Printed in the United States of America

ISBN 1-55622-843-0
10 9 8 7 6 5 4 3 2 1
0210

All inquiries for volume purchases of this book should be addressed to
Wordware Publishing, Inc., at 2320 Los Rios Boulevard, Plano, Texas 75074.
Telephone inquiries may be made by calling:

(972) 423-0090

Contents

Contents

Contents

Preface

I love stories, especially stories that bring out the human-interest aspects of real people and actual events. Besides providing entertainment, stories make people seem more real, and they make events more understandable. I love history, largely because of the stories that bring history to life.

This book is a book of stories. It is not to be considered a book of Texas history. Although intended to be entertaining, it might also serve as a supplement to a general overview of early Texas history. Every effort has been made to place the stories in their correct historical settings and to organize them into meaningful topical areas. Therefore, these stories, which focus on the humor and drama of the Texas frontier, are presented as being for the most part historically accurate.

I wish to thank Dr. Ray Stevens, retired professor of history at the University of North Texas and an expert in Texas history, for the many hours he spent reviewing a draft of this book and for his many helpful suggestions regarding facts and style. Any remaining errors are my own.

I also wish to thank my good wife, Billie, who has been an enthusiastic supporter of this project from its inception. Not only has she displayed great patience and understanding throughout the many hours I have spent collecting material and writing the stories, she has also read each story and has made many helpful suggestions. My love and my thanks go to Billie.

Hopefully, those who read this book will enjoy the stories as much as I have enjoyed collecting and writing them.

George U. Hubbard

Colonization

Introduction

T exas was touted as a land of opportunity, a land of promise, a land of "milk and honey." It was a land of wide-open
spaces, timbered forests, grassy prairies. It was a fertile
land where almost anything could be grown. It was a land
abounding in cattle, left over from the Spanish conquistadores,
that were free for the taking.

Colonization by Anglos from the United States began in
1821 with "Austin's 300." Having obtained title to a Mexican
land grant originally awarded to his father, Stephen F. Austin
brought in the first Anglo colonists and became known as the
"Father of Texas." Extending roughly 125 miles from Galveston
Bay to Matagorda Bay and about the same distance from the
Gulf coast inland to El Camino Real, the land route between
San Antonio and Nacogdoches, Austin's land grant became the
new home of over 1,200 colonists from the States.

From the time of Mexican independence from Spain, relationships between Mexico and the United States were strained,
largely because of a nebulous border that was very much in dispute. Thinking that Anglo colonists living under the laws and
authority of Mexico would constitute an effective buffer zone
between Mexico and the United States, the Mexican government encouraged such colonization and awarded many land
grants as inducements for more settlers. The lure of free, pro-
ductive land and free cattle in an area abounding with natural
resources brought thousands of settlers to Texas.

Advertisements in the East along with many personal testimonials had their effect, and Texans' legendary penchant for
bragging got an early start. In displays at the museum at Washington-on-the-Brazos, the following quotes illustrate this point.
Observer William Bollaert claimed Texas was a land so rich that
"if you plant tenpenny nails, you'll have a crop of iron bolts."

George Kendall, an 1840s journalist, considered the climate of Texas so healthy that he wrote, "If a man wants to die here, he must go somewhere else."

These glowing opinions were not universally shared, however. Tired of coping with the ticks, mosquitoes, sand flies, black mud, and other irritants, one colonist returned to the East commenting that Texas "is the most perfect purgatory of any place on Earth."

Still, the colonists kept coming!

What Happened to Our Ship?

Stephen F. Austin was discouraged. He had not been successful in attracting colonists to his father's land grants in Texas. He had wanted his colonists to "flock" to Texas, and flocking meant traveling on fast horses over passable roads. The horses were not available, the roads into Texas did not yet exist, and Austin was running short of funds. In a depressed state, Austin went to New Orleans in 1821 to visit a former college friend, the Honorable Joseph Hawkins.

After listening to Austin's discourse on the beauty and economic potential of Texas, Hawkins agreed to finance a few shiploads of colonists to Austin's colony on the Colorado River in Mexican Texas. They chartered the schooner *Lively* piloted by Captain Monroe, and on the appointed date, November 22, 1821, the *Lively* with a full complement of eighteen colonists as passengers left its berth in New Orleans. It was a gala morning as scores of people gathered at the pier to see the ship and its colonists depart. As Austin and Hawkins waved from the pier, the *Lively* started on its journey down the Mississippi River to the Gulf of Mexico and thence to Texas. Austin then went north

to Natchitoches, Louisiana, where he met another group of colonists who planned to travel on the *Lively's* second voyage to Texas.

Stephen F. Austin, New Orleans

Photo courtesy of Texas State Library & Archives Commission

4

The *Lively* never arrived at the Colorado River. Just off Galveston Island, the ship encountered a severe storm, and after being rocked and tossed by wind and waves, the distressed vessel managed to reach the mouth of the Brazos River about halfway between Galveston and the Colorado River. Casting anchor in the Brazos, the *Lively* discharged her cargo and underwent necessary repairs. About a week later Captain Monroe suddenly and mysteriously hoisted the ship's sails and sailed away, leaving all her passengers stranded ashore. Having no other recourse, the stranded colonists made their way up the river to a spot just west of present-day Houston where they founded the town of Richmond, said to be the first Anglo-Saxon town in Texas. Thus Stephen F. Austin succeeded in beginning a colony, but not in the planned location. Although the resourceful Austin found ways to continue the flow of colonists into Texas, most subsequent colonists traveled by land, not by sea.

Because of the *Lively's* sudden disappearance and the fact that it was never again seen in Texas, its fate became a widespread mystery among the Texas colonists. Many theories of the ship's fate were advanced, the most plausible being that Captain Monroe joined the pirate Jean Lafitte and spent some time plundering Spanish shipping in the Gulf of Mexico and the Caribbean Sea. The truth of the matter (determined years later) is that the *Lively* returned to New Orleans, picked up supplies and another group of colonists, and set sail again for Texas. This time the ship was wrecked at the western end of Galveston Island. Its passengers were rescued by the schooner *John Motely*, which landed them near the mouth of the Colorado River.

References:

Virgil N. Lott and Virginia M. Fenwick, *People and Plots on the Rio Grande* (San Antonio: The Naylor Company, 1957).

The New Handbook of Texas, Vol. 4 (Austin: The Texas State Historical Society, 1996).

Strap Buckner Goes One-Up on Stephen F. Austin

Students of Texas history are familiar with the name Stephen F. Austin, but it is likely that relatively few have heard of Aylette C. (Strap) Buckner. However, Strap is also deserving of a modicum of fame.

Strap Buckner was in Texas several years before Austin arrived with his colony. Coming from Virginia, Strap fought at Goliad in 1812 with the Gutierrez-Magee expedition. In 1821 he was one of the first to build a cabin on the Colorado River in what is now Fayette County. He was gregarious and entertained and fed all who passed his way, including Austin. But when Austin and his colony established civil government, Austin claimed lands that Strap considered his own by squatter's rights. Despite promises to the contrary, Austin wanted Strap's land and was determined to wrest control of it. And Strap was equally determined to resist. Trouble was on the horizon. Strap not only went to Matamoros, Mexico, seeking Mexican intervention, he also called a convention of settlers to protest against Austin's autocratic actions. So Austin decided that Strap must be arrested.

Now Strap was large and muscular, and his strength was legendary. Partly because of his fiery red hair, the neighboring Karankawa and Tonkawa Indians called him Kokulblothetoff, meaning Red Son of Blue Thunder. Strap was also good-natured, but when he patted people on the back, he frequently knocked them down. Smiling from ear to ear, he would edge into a circle of men and bowl them over like so many ninepins. One such friendly gesture severely injured one man, and Strap, feeling bad about it, nursed him back to health.

Because of his feats of strength, Strap's fame has grown to folklore proportions in Texas, and legend even has it that Strap once felled a charging bull with just his bare fist. But folklore is folklore, and Strap was a real person.

No one crossed Strap openly, and any attempt to arrest him was a task not to be desired. So when Stephen F. Austin ordered Andrew Rabb to arrest Strap for seditious conduct, Rabb conveniently became ill and remained so until Austin and Buckner reached their own settlement. If Buckner could not be subdued, perhaps his strengths could be used. Austin decided that a good relationship with Strap would be the wiser course. The two rivals finally settled their differences peaceably.

Strap kept the land he wanted to hold, and he became one of Austin's aides and military commanders. As Austin's emissary, Strap established a treaty of peace with the Waco and Tawakoni Indians near present-day Waco in the summer of 1824. As a military commander, Strap led an attack on the Karankawa Indians at Live Oak Bayou in 1831. It is said that Strap and Austin eventually became close friends. But all things must come to an end. The man whom Austin couldn't subdue was killed in the battle of Velasco on June 25, 1832. Strap's age at death is estimated to have been somewhere close to 43 years.

Reference:

Family records in the possession of the Jess Buckner family, Carlsbad, New Mexico.

Washington-on-the-Brazos Was a Wild and Free-Spirited River Town

Laid out in 1835 by John W. Hall, son-in-law of Andrew Robinson, one of "Austin's 300," the town of Washington played prominent roles in Stephen F. Austin's colony and in the subsequent Republic of Texas. Although only a small community today, Washington was initially a bustling shipping center on the lower Brazos River. It was also a very lively place, and in that respect, rather typical of other frontier towns of the period.

In 1840 Washington had approximately 350 inhabitants, of whom almost a hundred have been described as "principally gamblers, horse racers, etc." It has been said that in almost every other house on the public street, games of all sorts were played both night and day.

One British traveler to Washington noted that "the passion for erecting grog shops superseded the thirst for religious worship." As in other Texas towns, saloons outnumbered all other business enterprises.

Washington's economy centered on river transportation to the Gulf of Mexico, and the town served as a focal point for the shipping of exports and imports. The shipping, however, had its uncertainties and depended on the mood and water level of the Brazos River. Ships were frequently stranded by the low water, and at such times the crews of these stranded ships added an increased level of boisterousness to the environment of the area. One ship captain claimed that he could "tap a keg of beer and run his ship four miles on the suds." On the other hand, it is said that another stranded captain cleared and planted three hundred acres of corn while waiting for the river to rise.

Washington played two roles of special significance in Texas history. On March 2, 1836, delegates to the Independence Convention at Washington officially declared Texas to be independent of Mexico by signing a Declaration of Independence. Six years later, in 1842, President Sam Houston moved the capital of the Republic of Texas from Austin to Washington, following the occupation of San Antonio by a Mexican army.

Washington continued to prosper as long as river commerce was in vogue. But when the railroad built into nearby Brenham, Washington's decline began and was never reversed. Those interested in Texas history, however, will do well by visiting the excellent museum and outbuildings at present-day Washington-on-the-Brazos.

Reference:

Washington-on-the-Brazos Museum at Washington, Texas.

Davy Crockett Was the Hero, But His Wife Got the Monument

Davy Crockett was one of the heroes of the Alamo, but it is his wife, Elizabeth, for whom a monument was erected.

Davy was a widower and Elizabeth a widow when they married one another. As parents of five children by their previous marriages, they had three more of their own. Davy loved Elizabeth and got great pleasure jesting about her prowess as a frontier woman. In his writings, he portrayed Elizabeth as a female Paul Bunyan. "She has a bearskin petticoat and one dyed red with tiger's blood." Also, "Elizabeth could tell a bear from a panther in the dark by the feel of his bite."

Davy Crockett came to Texas in 1836 and joined the revolutionary movement. Elizabeth remained in Tennessee, looking westward for his return, but he never returned to Tennessee, having died a martyr at the Alamo.

Surrounded by the cemetery in Acton, Texas, Elizabeth's grave is situated on a separate state park of 0.006 acres, the smallest state

David Crockett

Photo courtesy of Texas State Library & Archives Commission

Monument to Elizabeth Crockett

Photo courtesy of Texas State Library & Archives Commission

park in Texas. In 1911 a majestic granite memorial marker was erected in the park. Atop the monument is a statue of Elizabeth looking west, just as she did for so long in Tennessee. Her martyred husband is still waiting for his monument.

References:

Ann Ruff, *Amazing Texas Monuments & Museums* (Houston: Lone Star Books, 1984).

The New Handbook of Texas, Vol. 1 (Austin: The Texas State Historical Society, 1996).

Flash Floods Sometimes Posed Special Challenges

Water could be a friend, and it could also be a foe. Many pioneer settlements were located on rivers or streams where dams could be built to provide water power for sawmills, gristmills, and irrigation. Dikes were also built to protect fields and crops from flooding. Flash floods from heavy rains and high water from melting snow frequently posed severe challenges by washing out many of these makeshift structures.

Many settlers had a hard time understanding that these western waterways with their sudden, violent discharges of water were very different from the more leisurely flowing streams in the East.

As one example, a settler from Iowa who had obtained a farm on the South Canadian River just south of Norman, Oklahoma, was laboring to build a dike to prevent flooding onto his land. A cowboy on the neighboring spread saw what was happening and asked the man, "What are you doing?"

"I'm building a dike to keep out the water," was the reply.

"Do you think it will work?" asked the cowboy.

"Why not? It's just like one I built in Iowa, and it worked there."

"Did you ask the river?" queried the cowboy.

The next time the river rose, it took out the dike and flooded half of the Iowan's field. Oklahoma streams were not just like Iowa streams.

Frequently dams and dikes would be washed out and have to be rebuilt. It could be a discouraging cycle, and sometimes whole settlements had to move on to other locations. And yet, it seemed as though divine providence occasionally interceded to avert complete tragedy.

Lyman Wight's millstone at Frontier Times Museum

Photo courtesy of G. U. Hubbard Collection

Lyman Wight and his Mormon colonists had several washouts in their central Texas settlements. Washed out at Austin, they moved to a location on the Pedernales River just northeast of Fredericksburg where they established the colony of Zodiac. There they erected a gristmill and a sawmill with which they not only provided for their own needs, but they also supplied lumber, cornmeal, and flour to the German colonists in that area. Their flour was especially fine as Lyman Wight had imported special millstones from France. But in 1851 raging flood waters in the Pedernales washed away both mills, and the Mormons were again left without means of subsistence. Worse, the millstones were lost as the torrent swept everything away.

Moving to Hamilton Creek, just south of Burnet, Wight's colony began another rebuilding effort. But a gristmill was impossible without millstones. They had to be located and recovered. Wight and a work party returned to the site of Zodiac, and as the story goes, Wight paced the riverbank and communed with the spirits until a revelation came to him. Then he went to a certain sandbar and pointed. "There!" he ordered. "Dig there."

Dig they did, and one can imagine how awestruck they were when their shovels struck and uncovered the lost millstones, exactly where Wight had pointed. A large portion of one of the recovered millstones is on display at the Frontier Times Museum at Bandera, Texas.

In another part of the West (the story is true, but the location has been forgotten) there is another example of the gods smiling favorably upon the settlers. In this colony the men had tried for several days in vain to erect a dam across their stream. Each morning they would find that their work of the previous day had been washed out. Discouraged and ready to move on, they tried one more time. When they went to look the next morning, not only was their partial construction still in place, but they saw signs of additions having been made. Perplexed, they nevertheless set to work again and completed their second day on the new dam. Again, the next morning more had been added.

The men finally caught on to what was happening. Somehow the beavers in the stream had gotten the idea that there was to be a dam in that location, and they had begun contributing their labors. So with the men working the day shift and the beavers working the night shift, a good solid dam was rapidly completed, and it had sufficient solidity to withstand the further onslaughts of the stream.

References:

Charles N. Gould, "Tales of an Oklahoma Geologist," *Folk-Say, A Regional Miscellany* (Norman: University of Oklahoma Press, 1930), B. A. Botkin, Ed.

Noah Smithwick, *The Evolution of a State* (Austin: University of Texas Press, 1984).

Mollie Heilman, "The Mormons Come to Texas," *The Texas Pioneer,* September-October 1931.

Three-Legged Willie Was Unusual in More Ways Than One

At the age of fifteen, Robert McAlpin Williamson contracted an illness that confined him to his bed for two years. Because the disease left him with a right knee permanently locked at a right angle, Williamson had to affix a wooden leg just below the immobilized knee. For the rest of his life, he was known as Three-Legged Willie.

Seeing the great potential of colonization in Texas, Williamson left his home in Georgia to join Stephen F. Austin's new colony at San Felipe. Along with his third leg that made him conspicuous wherever he went, Williamson brought several needed talents. He could speak six languages, and he was a lawyer. In addition to his judicial talents, Williamson was a gifted orator and was later called the "Patrick Henry of the Texas Revolution."

Robert McAlpin Williamson
(Three-Legged Willie)

Photo courtesy of Texas State Library & Archives Commission

15

In this capacity, his rangers served as a buffer between the advancing Mexican armies and Sam Houston's retreating Texians. Williamson personally joined Sam Houston's force at San Jacinto, riding into battle with long hair, matted and tangled beard, a suit of dirty buckskin, and a fur cap with nine dangling coon tails. It was facetiously said afterwards that Mexicans who saw him simply died of fright.

Williamson later became a district judge, a member of the Texas Supreme Court, and a legislator. As a judge in southeast Texas, he held many open-air court sessions under a spreading oak tree in Columbus. This was the best venue available at the time because the Texans, fleeing the advancing Mexicans in what became known as the Runaway Scrape, had burned most of Columbus rather than let it fall into Mexican hands. On their return from refuge in Louisiana following Houston's victory at San Jacinto, there was no appropriate indoor facility in Columbus for a courtroom, so Williamson used the shade of the giant oak tree.

One particular instance of Williamson's practical approach to judgeship is worth telling here. In Shelby County adjacent to the Louisiana border, no court had ever been held, and lawlessness was rampant. Going there to establish law and order and to end a long-standing feud, Williamson called a court session against the desires of many of the area's inhabitants. The session began with an ad hoc local lawyer placing a written resolution on the judge's table disavowing Williamson's jurisdiction over that area.

"What law or authority can you cite for such a proposal as this?" Williamson respectfully asked.

Drawing a Bowie knife from his belt and placing it on the paper, the ad hoc lawyer replied, "Your honor, this is the law in this country."

Then reaching under the long tail of his black coat, Williamson brought out the first six-shooter revolver the people there had ever seen, and laying it on top of the Bowie knife, proclaimed, "This is the Constitution that overrides the law. Sheriff, call the court to order."

Needless to say, Three-Legged Willie prevailed.

References:

Duncan W. Robinson, *Judge Robert McAlpin Williamson* (Austin: Texas State Historical Association, 1948).

John L. Davis, *The Texas Rangers* (San Antonio: Institute of Texan Cultures, 1991).

Independence

Introduction

M exico's plan for creating a buffer in the Nueces Strip between the Rio Grande and Nueces Rivers backfired. Although the colonists were initially quite willing to live under Mexican rule, the despotism and intolerance of many Mexican leaders, especially President Santa Anna, brought reactions of resistance from the free-spirited Anglo colonists.

As the first battles were fought, the Texians, as they called themselves, were fighting merely for the rights and benefits guaranteed by Mexico as conditions for their colonization. But as the severity of Mexican rule increased rather than moderating, independence became the goal of the Texians.

Within the Nueces Strip, coexistence of the two cultures proved unworkable. To the Texians, the Mexicans were an inferior people. The pursuit of free lands throughout all of Texas resulted in confiscating lands belonging to Mexican families as well as from the Indians. An almost constant state of agitation and belligerence existed between Anglos and Mexicans.

The challenge and expectation of open warfare brought a new wave of immigration from the United States into Texas. Home seekers sought economic opportunity, adventurers came for action, and a lawless element wanted to escape likely punishment and confinement. The new immigrants came to fight, and Texas became the setting for conflict. As the fighting progressed, it appeared that the numerically superior Mexican forces would overwhelm the smaller and less organized Texian forces, and for the most part, this is the way the battles went.

The tide finally turned, however, and Texas won its independence when Sam Houston's army defeated Santa Anna's forces at San Jacinto on April 21, 1836. But even after independence, border disputes continued for many years with both nations making claim on the Nueces Strip. Mexican armies made several forays across the Rio Grande, and in 1842, the Mexican army advanced twice as far north as San Antonio before being driven back. Although a definite border was established and recognized as a result of the Mexican War of 1846-48, skirmishes within the Strip continued for many more years.

Texas Colonists React to Oppression

It is ironic that John D. Bradburn, an American in the service of Mexico, is credited with igniting the spark that ultimately led to Texas independence.

Spending his earlier life as a merchant in Columbia, Tennessee, Bradburn augmented his income by stealing slaves and selling them in neighboring states. Caught in the act on one occasion in 1828, Bradburn was jailed, but he cut himself out using a file smuggled in to him by a confederate. Making his way to Mexico, Bradburn spent the rest of his life as a Mexican official, antagonistic toward the gringos. Marrying a titled heiress, Maria Josefa Hurtado de Mendoza, Bradburn performed many services for the Mexican government and rose to the rank of lieutenant colonel in the Mexican militia.

Bradburn's antagonism toward the Americans showed itself most strongly in 1832 when he established a fort and a customhouse at Perry's Point (renamed Anahuac after the ancient capital of the Aztecs) on Trinity Bay in Texas.

As commander of the Mexican forces at Anahuac, Bradburn issued repressive orders and arrogantly demanded strict obedience from the colonists. This made him very unpopular among the Texians, who were not people to be pushed around. One of Bradburn's more unpopular moves was in establishing the customs station for collecting fees and duties from the colonists and from nearby shipping.

Relationships between Mexico and the Texas colonists were already strained. President Vicente Guerrero abolished slavery in 1829, and he followed this unpopular move in 1830 by banning further American immigration into Texas and by canceling the Texians' exemptions from Mexican fees and duties. And now Bradburn's hated customs station was taking money and resources sorely needed by the colonists.

Further fuel was added to the fire by the presence of a popular young lawyer, William B. Travis, from Alabama. Travis and his law partner, Patrick C. Jack, had been retained to recover two runaway slaves who were in Bradburn's garrison. Bradburn and the hotheaded Travis clashed almost immediately, and Bradburn sought to end that difficulty by arresting both Travis and Jack and incarcerating them in an empty brick kiln. But when Bradburn threatened to send his prisoners to Vera Cruz where they would probably be executed, the colonists rose up in defense of Travis and Jack.

On June 10, 1832, a rebel force of colonists invaded Anahuac and captured Bradburn's entire force of nineteen cavalrymen. Bradburn agreed to release Travis, Jack, and other Anglo prisoners in exchange for his nineteen soldiers, provided all the rebels would leave the town. The rebels released the cavalrymen, but when Bradburn learned that some of the rebels were still in Anahuac, he refused to release his prisoners. The rebels then withdrew to Turtle Bayou, a few miles north of Anahuac, drew up a series of resolutions expressing their complaints against Bradburn, and prepared for further battle.

About two weeks after the initial engagement, Henry Smith and John Austin led a group of men to Brazoria, near the mouth

of the Brazos River, to obtain a cannon for use at Anahuac. Returning to Anahuac on a small confiscated steamboat, they attacked and defeated a Mexican garrison at Velasco that was blocking their way. When fighting again broke out at Anahuac, Colonel Jose de las Piedras, Bradburn's superior officer, came down from Nacogdoches to put an end to the hostilities.

Stephen F. Austin monument at Texas State Cemetery

Photo courtesy of G. U. Hubbard Collection

23

Acceding to the colonists' demands, Piedras freed Travis and Jack on July 2, and eleven days later, Piedras removed Bradburn from his command. The victorious colonists gave Bradburn twenty-four hours to disappear, and he was smart enough not to require all that time. Bradburn made his way to New Orleans and then back to Mexico.

These battles are commonly acknowledged as the first military engagements in liberating Texas from Mexico. They occurred because of the overbearing despotism of an American with misplaced loyalties.

———————————

References:

Virgil N. Lott and Virginia M. Fenwick, *People and Plots on the Rio Grande* (San Antonio: The Naylor Company, 1957).

David G. McComb, *Texas: A Modern History* (Austin: University of Texas Press, 1989).

Margaret Swett Hensen, *Juan Davis Bradburn: A Reappraisal of the Mexican Commander of Anahuac* (College Station: Texas A&M University Press, 1982).

The New Handbook of Texas, Vol. 3 (Austin: The Texas State Historical Association, 1996).

Much Ado About Grass

In November 1835 the Texians got word of a large shipment of silver en route by pack mules from Mexico to San Antonio to pay the Mexican soldiers of General Martin Perfecto de Cos that were stationed there. Not only did the Texians want to prevent such payment, they also felt the desirability of using the silver for their own purposes. So on the morning of November 28 when Erastus (Deaf) Smith spotted a large pack train, guarded by 150 Mexican *soldados*, approaching San Antonio, excitement reigned among the Texians who were camped just outside of San Antonio. Surely the Mexican silver would soon become Texian silver.

The Texians, led by Colonel Edward Burleson, quickly mustered and prepared themselves for battle, which took place about a mile outside of San Antonio. Burleson ordered James Bowie and 40 cavalrymen to lead the way, with William A. Jack to follow with about 100 infantry. Racing toward the Mexican pack train, Bowie encountered them head-on as the Mexicans were crossing a dry creek bed. The Mexicans scattered along the creek bed, and Bowie and his men took cover in another creek bed nearby and repelled at least four Mexican attempts to dislodge them. Jack and his force soon arrived on the scene, as did Mexican artillery and reinforcements sent from San Antonio by Colonel Cos. The fierce fighting ended when Texian reinforcements under James Swisher arrived. The Mexicans decided it was time to seek the safety of a haven in San Antonio.

Having won the battle, the Texians rushed to the abandoned pack train and began opening the bags carried by the animals. One can image their surprise and bewilderment as they picked up the captured packs and found them much too light to contain silver coins and bullion. Opening the first pack, they found it full of grass. One by one each of the remaining packs yielded the same "treasure." The Mexicans had simply gone out the night before and cut a large amount of grass, which they were bringing back to their fort to feed to their horses.

At a cost of four men wounded and seventeen Mexicans dead or wounded, the Texians now had a goodly supply of grass for their own horses. What about the shipment of silver? No one remembers.

Historian J. R. Edmondson, in *The Alamo Story*, commented that this ludicrous engagement, which became mockingly known as the Grass Fight, was significant in at least one major way. It energized a majority of Texian soldiers and helped unify what previously had been a rather disorganized army of fighters.

References:

D. W. C. Baker, *A Texas Scrap-book* (New York: A. S. Barnes & Company, 1875).

J. R. Edmondson, *The Alamo Story* (Plano: Republic of Texas Press, 2000).

Alwyn Barr, *Texans in Revolt: The Battle for San Antonio, 1835* (Austin: University of Texas Press, 1990).

The New Handbook of Texas, Vol. 3 (Austin: The Texas State Historical Association, 1996).

Texans Rally in Remembering the Alamo and Goliad

In 1836 Mexican armies scored significant victories over the Texians (as they were called) at the Alamo and at Goliad in campaigns that were in sharp contrast to one another. While the heroic defense of the Alamo by gallant men who died in battle served to rally the beleaguered Texian forces, the treacherous slaughter of defenseless Texians at Goliad angered the Anglos, causing deep-seated desires for revenge.

The story of San Antonio's Alamo and its gallant defense by a small band under Colonel William Travis's leadership is well known. The 189 defenders at the Alamo were expecting to be reinforced by Colonel James Fannin and his 400 men, but Fannin was occupied in the Goliad area, about 80 miles to the southeast. Immediately following the tragic defeat at the Alamo, General Sam Houston ordered Fannin and his men to retreat from Goliad to Victoria. In attempting to make their departure, Fannin and his forces were overtaken at Coleto Creek by a numerically superior Mexican army, which forced them to surrender. They were imprisoned in the Presidio

The garrison chapel at La Bahia in Goliad

Photo courtesy of Western History Collections, University of Oklahoma Libraries

Nuestra Señora Santa María de Loreto de la Bahía del Espíritu Santo at Goliad.

Despite promises of safe and humane treatment, which were conditions for their surrender, Santa Anna ordered the execution of all of Fannin's forces. Thus, on the morning of Palm Sunday in 1836, as about 380 Texians were marching out in three groups for a work detail, the guards began firing at their prisoners, killing 352 of them. The last to die was Colonel Fannin who, while too ill to join his men, was executed in the presidio.

A few of the Texians managed to escape the execution. A Mexican woman referred to as "The Angel of Goliad" succeeded in hiding twenty-five, and another thirty escaped death by running away.

The Mexicans stripped the bodies of the slain men, then partially burned them and left them unburied. Nine weeks later, when General Thomas J. Rusk arrived at Goliad with a Texas army, the exposed corpses were carried to an appropriate burial site and given a military funeral on June 3, 1836.

As a result of these two tragedies, two battle cries were born at the subsequent Battle of San Jacinto: "Remember the Alamo" and "Remember Goliad" (or "Remember la Bahía"). These two battle cries became rallying cries as they spurred Sam Houston's forces to victory over Santa Anna's Mexican army at San Jacinto.

References:

Claude Dooley and Betty Dooley, *Why Stop? A Guide to Texas Historical Roadside Markers* (Houston: Gulf Publishing Company, 1985).

David G. McComb, *Texas: A Modern History* (Austin: University of Texas Press, 1999).

The Capture of General Santa Anna

The battle was over. Sam Houston and his band of Texians had defeated Santa Anna's Mexican army at the Battle of San Jacinto, and Texas had essentially won its independence from Mexico. Throughout the remainder of the day and into the night, the Texians hunted the scattered Mexicans. Some were brought in as prisoners; many others were slaughtered.

The next day an air of relaxation settled on Houston's forces as they licked their wounds and began to forage the area around the San Jacinto battlefield for food and game. During the course of the afternoon, surviving Mexican prisoners were processed, and many were subsequently set free to return to their native land. But General Santa Anna was nowhere to be found, neither among the prisoners nor among the dead, and this greatly disturbed Sam Houston. Although the Texians had won the battle, if Santa Anna were free to organize another army, the Texians might not yet have won the war.

As Joel Robinson and a patrol of four other Texians were foraging near the destroyed Vince's Bayou Bridge about five miles away from the battle site, they happened upon a lone Mexican soldier concealed in a thicket. Wearing a white blouse and trousers that resembled a Mexican fatigue uniform, the soldier had become disoriented in attempting to escape and had hidden in the thicket all night following the battle. Upon hearing the Texians approach, he attempted to further conceal himself under a blanket. The Texians discovered him, however, and Robinson managed to prevail over the other Texians who wanted to shoot the prisoner.

Tempted at first to let the bedraggled warrior go, Robinson thought the better of it and ordered the captive onto his (Robinson's) horse. As the patrol approached the Texian encampment, Robinson was again tempted to let the polite little Mexican go free. But when he noticed some of the Mexican prisoners saluting the captive seated behind him on his horse, Robinson got the idea that perhaps his captive was no ordinary prisoner. As the patrol continued into the encampment center, other Mexican prisoners raised their hats and began the shout, "El Presidente, El Presidente!" The captain of the guard came running, and the prisoner gave Robinson the shock of his life by requesting to be taken directly to General Houston.

And thus it was that Santa Anna, the general of the defeated Mexican army and dictator of the Mexican nation, was captured and surrendered personally to Sam Houston the day following the Battle of San Jacinto.

References:

E. G. Littlejon, *Texas History Stories* (Richmond: B. F. Johnson Publishing Co., 1901).

David G. McComb, *Texas: A Modern History* (Austin: University of Texas Press, 1999).

Drawing a Black Bean Meant Death

A few years after Texas gained its independence at San Jacinto and General Santa Anna was released, the Mexican general again became president of Mexico. Ignoring his promise to refrain from further hostilities, Santa Anna continuously threatened to retake Texas. In September 1842, a Mexican army unit commanded by General Adrian Woll captured San Antonio. Texans immediately rallied to the call and, after intense combat, forced the Mexican army to retreat below the Rio Grande.

The Texans, under the command of General Alexander Somervell, gave chase, marched to the Rio Grande, and captured Laredo. Somervell, however, refused to let his relatively small force cross over into Mexico where a larger enemy force awaited. Three hundred of the pursuing force ignored Somervell's order to return to their homes, and this small band, under Colonel William S. Fisher, continued down the Rio Grande to the Mexican town of Mier. Crossing the river on Christmas Eve in a driving rain, they entered the town and gave battle to the Mexican contingent camped there. With losses on both sides, the fighting was heavy until the Mexican general Ampudia asked for a brief truce.

Execution of those who drew black beans

Photo courtesy of The Center for American History, The University of Texas

31

Ampudia told the Texans that 800 fresh Mexican troops were due to arrive. If the Texans would surrender now, he promised they would soon be on their way home after prisoner exchanges. Colonel Fisher advised the Texans to submit. "Ampudia is a man of his word. He can be trusted." But Ampudia was not a man of his word, and soon the Texans found themselves embarking on a 1,000-mile march to Mexico City, flanked on either side by Mexican guards with fixed bayonets.

Arriving at the town of Salado on February 10, 1843, the Texans decided to make a break for freedom. The next morning at breakfast they overpowered their guards, captured and mounted horses, and set out for freedom and home. Traveling in unfamiliar and desolate country, they lost their way and ran out of food. They were on the verge of starvation when they found themselves surrounded by a Mexican detachment commanded by General Mexia. The kindly general gave them a few days to recover their strength and then marched them back to Salado.

Word came from Santa Anna that all the prisoners should be put to death. By correspondence, General Mexia and others pled with Santa Anna to spare and release the Texans. Their efforts achieved partial results, as Santa Anna softened his orders to the effect that one tenth of the Texans be shot.

On the appointed day, one of the Mexican officers approached the Texans with an earthen pot containing 159 white beans and 17 black beans. Those Texans drawing the black beans would be the ones to die. The commissioned officers were ordered to draw first, followed by the enlisted men in alphabetical order by last name.

Captain Ewen Cameron, who was to make the initial draw, had noticed that the Mexicans had put the white beans into the pot first and then put the black beans on top without mixing them. He whispered to his fellow officers, "Dig deep, boys." Cameron drew out a white bean as did every other officer except Captain Eastland.

William A. A. "Bigfoot" Wallace was one of the last to draw a bean, and the remaining whites and blacks were well mixed by that time. Wallace, however, thought he had observed that the black beans were slightly larger than the white. Acting on this assumption, he fingered the beans in the jar, and with two remaining in his hand, he drew out the smaller. It was white, and Wallace survived another of many ordeals in his colorful life.

At sundown the selected prisoners were tied, blindfolded, and made to sit down on a log. The fateful command was given, and the deed was done. Sixteen Texans died immediately, and one, James L. Shepherd, was merely wounded. Pretending death, Shepherd lay still until after dark when he got up and escaped into the night. A few weeks later he was captured and killed by the Mexicans. Captain Cameron, who had drawn the first white bean, was also executed by the Mexicans following a later escape attempt.

Five years after the black bean episode, the remains of the slaughtered were dug up and reburied at La Grange, Texas, where a large monument erected by the state of Texas marks their last resting place.

References:

E. G. Littlejon, *Texas History Stories* (Richmond: B. F. Johnson Publishing Co., 1901).

John C. Duval, *Adventures of Big Foot Wallace* (Omaha: University of Nebraska Press, 1966).

Thomas J. Green, *Journal of the Texian Expedition Against Mier* (New York: Arno Press, 1973).

Sam W. Haynes, *Soldiers of Misfortune* (Austin: University of Texas Press, 1990).

Juan Cortina Was a Hero to the Mexicans

Mexican-born Juan Cortina grew up in the Nueces Strip at a time when the Strip was claimed by both Mexico and the United States. Because of its uncertain political status, this "no-man's land" between the Rio Grande and Nueces River attracted numerous entrepreneurs and scalawags who came to profit from the situation. In that environment, the red-bearded Cortina learned to hate the Anglos, especially land-grabbers who robbed Mexican families, including Cortina's mother, of their properties. Charlie Stillman, of Brownsville, was a local political boss and land-grabber whom Cortina particularly hated.

Cortina became somewhat of a gang leader, leading raids throughout the area and killing several Anglos in the process. In July 1859 Stillman hired Bob Shears as city marshal with a charge to go out and arrest Cortina and his gang. Prudently waiting for Cortina to come to him, Shears got his opportunity on July 13. Coming into Brownsville, Cortina and three of his men went into a cantina near Market Plaza, and another of his men, Pedro Juarado, went into a saloon across the street. Sending word to his deputies to come muy pronto, Shears decided to start with the lone man in the saloon, Juarado, but as he went in, Cortina saw from across the street what was about to happen. In a flash, Cortina dashed outside, mounted his big stallion, and rode right into the saloon. Shears, in the process of disarming Juarado, didn't have a chance. Firing twice, Cortina brought Shears down. Then scooping up Juarado, Cortina rode his horse back out through the bat-wing doors and into the plaza where he shattered the plate glass window of Stillman's office with another shot.

The posse refused to take action, so another posse was recruited under the sheriff, a man named Brown, who was also

34

a longtime friend of Cortina. Going with this new posse to Cortina's stronghold at Rancho Santa Rita, about seven miles out of Brownsville, Sheriff Brown had to confront Cortina alone as the posse refused to ride onto the property. After a friendly exchange of words, Cortina refused to come to Brownsville to be tried by Stillman's judge and jury. Sheriff Brown went back to Brownsville empty-handed.

Over the next few weeks, men flocked to Cortina by the hundreds. Mexicans, Anglo sympathizers, and adventurers in general joined his growing band, anxious to wreak vengeance on the oppressors of the defenseless Mexican families in the Strip. Cortina had a list of land-grabbers with whom he wanted to deal personally, and because the citizens of Brownsville would not deliver these people to him, he invaded the town in October of 1859. Cortina and his band captured Fort Brown from the U.S. Cavalry, occupied the city hall and all other government buildings, and methodically sacked the city. Cortina particularly wanted to find the designated land-grabbers, but they had already fled the area.

The Americans in Brownsville frantically appealed to General Alejandro Carvajal and his Mexican forces across the Rio Grande, and they came to the rescue. Retreating to his Rancho Santa Rita, Cortina successfully fought off an attempt by Texas Rangers to subdue him. Companies of volunteers were formed in several Texas towns, and the U.S. Army ordered Brevet-Colonel Robert E. Lee to take command of all these forces. Before Lee could do so, however, his orders were changed and he was sent to Harper's Ferry, in what is now West Virginia, to take command in the John Brown affair. Lee returned to Texas in early 1860 and organized an unsuccessful pursuit of Cortina.

In a battle with the combined U.S. forces, Cortina and his men were again the victors. Then marching northward, Cortina captured Edinburg and then Rio Grande City on Christmas Eve, 1859. On the following day, Christmas Day, Cortina made the mistake of ordering a fiesta for his men. While they consumed barbecue and mescal, over a thousand U.S. soldiers and Texas Rangers struck the unprepared band and thoroughly decimated them. Cortina and a small number of survivors fled to safety across the Rio Grande. From his new headquarters on the

Mexican side of the river, Cortina and his men made sporadic raids into the United States, stealing thousands of head of cattle before Captain Lee McNelly and another group of Texas Rangers permanently broke up the band fifteen years later in 1875.

Despite being overcome by the Anglos, Cortina remained a hero to the Mexicans throughout the ensuing years. He was elected mayor of Matamoros and then governor of the Mexican state of Tamaulipas. He won further fame by fighting against the French puppet Maximilian. Aspiring to become president of Mexico, he was finally beaten by his first cousin, Porfirio Diaz. Juan Cortina is still remembered on both sides of the Rio Grande.

References:

Ruel McDaniel, "Juan Cortina—Hero or Bandit?," *True West*, September-October 1956.

David G. McComb, *Texas: A Modern History* (Austin: University of Texas Press, 1999).

Indians

Introduction

The Indians were here first. This was their land. But westward expansion under the justification of "Manifest Destiny" was not to stop until the Americans reached the Pacific Ocean.

Although efforts were made on both sides to coexist peacefully, it was not to be. Indians of the Great Plains were nomadic, following the buffalo up and down the country. As the white men usurped the lands and built roads and erected fences, it was not just a matter of restricting the Indian's way of life, it was a matter of destroying a whole culture. Indian resistance was only natural.

Raids, thievery, and murders by the Indians became an expected part of frontier life, and the whites defended themselves and retaliated as necessary. Scalping of their victims was considered to be a unique Indian custom although the Europeans practiced scalping during the French-Indian War. The act of scalping was a guarantee that the spirit of the victim would be dispatched down to the Indian version of hell.

Although several tribes existed on the Texas landscape, the Comanches were the most troublesome to the whites. The Comanches especially hated the white surveyors who were considered to be forerunners of further white expansion into their precious lands. As fierce fighters and excellent horsemen, the Comanches raided settlements and committed atrocities that generated retaliatory actions by the whites. Gradually the whites predominated, but organized hostilities continued until Quanah Parker, the last of the great Comanche war chiefs, walked into Fort Sill, Oklahoma, in 1875.

Along with murdering the whites, the Comanches liked to kidnap white women and children. These they could sell to other tribes or keep for themselves. In more than one case, the captives assimilated into the Comanche way of life and resisted efforts to be brought back to white civilization. Cynthia Ann Parker, the mother of Quanah Parker, was the most famous of these converts.

The White Man's Ways Were Not the Indians' Ways

The lifestyles of the white men and the Plains Indians were so vastly different from each other that coexistence in the same geographical areas was an impossible concept. The white men lived in cabins or houses permanently located on land they owned or rented. They raised crops and they built fences to restrict the movement of domestic livestock and wild game. On the other hand, the nomadic Plains Indians lived off the game of the land, and they dwelt in movable shelters so they could follow the migrations of the game. They had no concept of private property or of land ownership.

Chief Muguara of the Comanches expressed the situation succinctly to Noah Smithwick: "We have set up our lodges in these groves and swung our children from these boughs from time immemorial. When game moves away from us we pull down our lodges and move away, leaving no trace to frighten it, and in a little while it comes back. But the white man comes and cuts down the trees, building houses and fences, and the buffalos get frightened and leave and never come back, and the Indians are left to starve, or, if we follow the game, we trespass on the hunting ground of other tribes and war ensues."

A herd of buffalo on the plains

Photo courtesy of Western History Collections, University of Oklahoma Libraries

40

Satanta, the Kiowa chieftain who was sometimes referred to as the "Orator of the Plains," expressed similar viewpoints on a number of occasions. With regard to domesticating himself in a house, Satanta absolutely refused. "This building homes for us is all nonsense. Time enough to build us houses when the buffalo are all gone; but tell the Great Father that there are plenty of buffalo yet."

The roving herds of buffalo constituted the primary means of sustenance and support for the Plains Indians, and geographic restrictions and wholesale killing of the beasts were unthinkable. Angered over the white man's wanton destruction of the buffalo, Satanta cried out on another occasion, "Why do you kill and not eat?"

Quanah Parker, the great Comanche war chief, similarly resisted assimilation by the whites until finally resigning himself to the inevitable. As the last Comanche chief to surrender to reservation life, Parker came to the realization that the Indians must either adopt the white man's ways or be destroyed. In later life he built a large home, acquired large herds of cattle, and entered into a variety of business ventures. Quanah Parker became wealthy, financed the building of a railroad, and generally outsmarted the white men at their own games. But Quanah Parker was the exception rather than the rule. Generally speaking, trying to mix the two vastly different cultures was no more successful than trying to mix oil and water.

When Smithwick suggested allotting land to the Comanches and furnishing them with means to cultivate it, Muguara emphatically rejected the suggestion. "The Indians were not made to work. If they build houses and try to live like white men, they will die." Then he added, "If the white men would draw a line defining their claims and keep on their side of it, the red men would not molest them."

Although Smithwick saw the futility of trying to draw such a line, he escorted five Comanche chiefs to the Texas capital at Houston to formally make such a request of President Sam Houston. After listening to the Indian pleas, Houston sadly shook his head, saying. "If I could build a wall from the Red River to the Rio Grande, so high that no Indian could scale it, the white people would go crazy trying to devise means to get

41

beyond it." The five chiefs knew that Houston was right, and with equal sadness, they withdrew their request.

Satanta, Kiowa Chief

Thinking that a show of strength could be a deterrent to further warfare, Sam Houston sought to impress the five chiefs by showing the resources of the white men. They visited the armory where guns, cannon, and munitions were stored, and they visited a steamboat at a wharf on the bayou. The Indians had never before seen anything like a steamboat, and they were very impressed and also fearful of it. President Houston told them that the Americans had hundreds of them and could make them run on land just as easily as on water. The Indians, naively, had no basis for not believing such a claim.

Returning to their settlements, the Indian chiefs had been truly impressed by the strength of the white men. They were also saddened at prospects for the future. Everyone knew that the nomadic way of life of the Plains Indians and the domesticated way of life of the white people could not and would not blend together.

References:

Carl Coke Rister, *No Man's Land* (Norman: University of Oklahoma Press, 1948).

Noah Smithwick, *The Evolution of a State* (Austin: University of Texas Press, 1984).

A Lipan Indian Chief Weeps Openly over the Loss of a Son

The Lipan Apache Indians of central Texas were a proud but docile group, although they could fight fiercely when pressed. Bitter enemies of the more savage Comanches, the Lipans allied themselves with the white settlers for protection and for trade. In early 1839 a party of Lipans discovered a Comanche encampment just north of what is now Austin. Not wanting to attack alone and knowing that equal enmity existed between the whites and the Comanches, the Lipans returned to the white settlements and gave the alarm. If the whites would attack, the Lipans would assist.

The settlements of La Grange and Bastrop raised about thirty men each, and in company with the Lipans, they went after the hated Comanches. One of the Lipan commanders was a young leader named Flacco, son of the elderly Flacco, the Lipan chief. Captain William M. Eastland led the La Grange contingent, and Noah Smithwick commanded the men from Bastrop. Colonel John Henry Moore was the overall commander of the expedition.

In the meantime, the Comanches had moved northward to the San Gabriel River. Snow and sleet delayed the march and forced the pursuers to seek shelter in a grove of post oaks. Some of their horses froze to death, and the Lipans, not as proud as the whites, feasted on the horsemeat. A rifle that had been propped against a tree fell and discharged, killing one of the La Grange men. Things were not going well for the pursuers.

Eventually the Lipans and their allies reached the Comanche camp and quietly surrounded it in the night. The Comanches were much more numerous than expected, and Colonel Moore hesitated to attack. One big, rough fellow said, "I don't care if there are a thousand of them, if there are enough horses to justify the fight." With this as a rallying cry, the attack

43

began, and the Comanches were taken completely by surprise. Pandemonium ensued with the Comanche men bounding from their lodges and scattering like partridges. Women and children were screaming and dogs were barking as the men were yelling and shooting. It was virtually a complete rout when, for reasons never explained, Colonel Moore ordered a retreat. This gave the Comanches time to regroup, and from that point on, the battle was a standoff.

One Comanche, wounded and lying flat on his back, repeatedly shot arrows into the attacking group. The young Flacco distinguished himself by charging out amid a rain of arrows and killing the wounded Comanche with a lance. Flacco took the Comanche's shield but was forced to retreat before getting his scalp.

Young Flacco, the idol of his tribe, was unswerving in his loyalty to the whites. In honor of his many services, the Texas government bestowed upon him the title of "colonel" and presented him with a full colonel's uniform complete with a sword and a plumed, cockaded hat. He learned enough English to call himself Flacco Colonel.

In the summer of 1842, the young Flacco was hired to accompany an expedition of the U.S. Army against Mexico. Flacco and a deaf Lipan brave served as scouts and led the way honorably in many engagements along the Rio Grande. As the expedition returned following the hostilities, the deaf Indian became sick, and he and Flacco paused at the Medina River as the white men continued homeward. While thus encamped, they were attacked and murdered by a band of Mexicans.

When two white men were seen in Seguin with Flacco's horses, Smithwick, a close friend of the old Chief Flacco, was afraid that the chief would blame the whites for the tragedy and seek revenge. Chief Flacco, on the other hand, sought to avoid turning against the whites, and at his request, messages were sent to General Sam Houston and to Senor Antonio Navarro seeking their understanding of the affair. Both corroborated the true situation, Houston sent his sympathy to the old chief and the tribe, and the long-standing friendship with the whites was preserved.

It was at this point that the old chief departed from the usual stoicism of Indian demeanor. Normally, an Indian warrior would not be guilty of such weakness as to weep. But Smithwick reports that "tears rained down the old man's face while sobs fairly shook his frame."

"It has always been our custom," the old man said, "to destroy everything belonging to the dead, but my son was the white man's friend and I want to do with his things as white men do." He then offered several items including a rawhide box in which the young Flacco had kept his colonel's uniform. Insisting that the chief keep the uniform and give other offered items to Flacco's young friends, Smithwick politely declined to accept the gifts. A few days later, however, four horses, one of which had been caught and trained for Sam Houston, were delivered to Smithwick.

What might have been a volatile situation between the Lipans and the whites was diplomatically defused. Peaceful relations were maintained between the whites and an old chief who wept openly and without embarrassment for his deceased son.

Reference:

Noah Smithwick, *The Evolution of a State* (Austin: University of Texas Press, 1984).

Enchanted Rock was Sacred to the Indians

Enchanted Rock, located eighteen miles north of Fredericksburg on the highway to Llano, had a special and sacred meaning to the Indian tribes of central Texas. It was considered to be holy ground, and sacred rites were performed within its shadows. This is not a unique phenomenon. Stone Mountain in Georgia has similar spiritual connotations, as does Ayers Rock, which is sacred to the Aborigines of Australia.

On the other hand, Enchanted Rock has become a modern mecca for tourists and rock climbers. From the top of this rock of pure pink granite, one obtains a commanding view of the surrounding countryside for miles around. The panoramic vistas of cardinal-red Indian blankets and indigo bluebonnets, interspersed with ribbons of oak, hickory, and mesquite trees, can be exhilarating. The several varieties of cacti and colored lichens add local interest and beauty. Bird watching is also a popular activity for many of the 300,000 people who visit the rock each year.

Diorama of Jack Hays on Enchanted Rock at Texas Ranger Museum

Photo courtesy of G. U. Hubbard Collection

Enchanted Rock is a single stone monolith 425 feet in height. Actually it is a large bump on a much larger granite deposit that covers about 100 square miles and which was formed of molten rock some seven miles underground.

Although very little is known of the religious connotations with which the Indians regarded the rock, archaeologists have unearthed dozens of archaic Indian sites in and around Enchanted Rock. Perhaps as far back as 10,000 years, groups of hunters and gatherers left hunting and fishing tools such as notched dart points, which were used to tip short spears. About A.D. 900 the hunters improved their technique by using bows and arrows. Arrow points along with shards of pottery have also been unearthed.

Jack Hays: Texas Ranger Captain

Photo courtesy of Western History Collections, University of Oklahoma Libraries

One incident, involving Captain John Coffee "Jack" Hays, a former professional surveyor turned Texas Ranger, hints at the sacred nature of Enchanted Rock although the incident also reflects the Comanches' feelings towards white surveying parties. The Comanches hated surveyors; to the Comanches, the presence of surveyors on their lands meant the subsequent loss of additional land to the ever-expanding white settlements. Therefore, when a band of Comanches discovered Hays and a party of about twenty men surveying land near the head of the Pedernales River in the fall of 1841, trouble was to be expected.

As the surveying party approached the Enchanted Rock area, Hays strayed off alone and encountered three Comanche Indians who began chasing him with the intent to kill. Not only were the whites seen as preparing to wrest additional land from the open range, but now it was sacred land that was in jeopardy.

As there was a large camp of Comanches nearby, Hays raced to the nearest place of refuge, Enchanted Rock itself. With his life in jeopardy, Hays obtained safety by scrambling to the top of the rock. One account says he managed to spur his horse to the top. Rather than compounding such a desecration, some of the Comanches declined to follow. But to others of the Indians, Hays was a pollutant to their sacred monument, and they tried to dislodge him. From his secluded position at the top, Hays occasionally fired at the Comanches, killing four or five of them.

Remaining at the top, Hays maintained a standoff against the Comanches until the armed surveying party arrived to rescue their leader and put the Comanches to flight.

Enchanted Rock, now a National Natural Landmark, is open to tourists and campers and is still sacred ground to the Indians of Texas.

References:

Harry McCorry Henderson, *Colonel Jack Hays, Texas Ranger* (San Antonio: The Naylor Co., 1954).

Janet R. Edwards, "The Hill Country's Rock of Ages," *Texas Highways*, March 2000.

Richard Zelade, *Hill Country* (Houston: Gulf Publishing Company, 1997).

General Sherman Was Closer to Death Than He Realized

Were the Indian uprisings in Texas really as bad as they were being portrayed? In May 1871 General William Tecumseh Sherman, Civil War general and now senior military officer of the United States, went to Texas on an inspection trip to find out for himself.

Passing through Salt Creek Prairie on their way to Fort Richardson (outside of Jacksboro), Sherman and his party unknowingly passed by a party of over one hundred Indians led by Kiowa chiefs Satanta, Satank, and Big Tree. The Indians, consisting of warriors of the Kiowa, Comanche, Arapaho, and Cheyenne tribes, were on the warpath, having left their reservations for a big raid in Texas. The three chiefs watched the Sherman party pass by but decided not to attack them only because Maman-ti, the Owl Prophet, claimed that there would be two parties of white men and the second party would be easier prey.

The next day Sherman came to the realization of how close he had been to death when he heard news that a second party had indeed followed and had been massacred at Salt Creek. A wounded teamster of the Warren wagon train made his way to Fort Richardson and reported the deaths of seven members of the party. Five others had escaped. An inspection of the site revealed that all of the dead had been riddled with bullets, skulls had been smashed, and one man had his tongue cut out.

Sherman immediately ordered Colonel Ranald S. Mackenzie to lead an all-out pursuit after the Indians. After burying the massacred bodies, Mackenzie followed the marauders' trail to Fort Sill.

In the meantime, the Indians returned to their reservation where Satanta boasted of the deed, saying that any other chief who claimed the honor was a liar. The Indian agent persuaded

Satanta, Satank, and Big Tree to come into Fort Sill peaceably to meet with General Sherman, who thereupon ordered their arrest. When Mackenzie arrived at Fort Sill, he was amazed to find his culprits already there behind bars.

As Mackenzie began his journey to Jacksboro for the trial of the Kiowa leader in a Texas state court, Satank attempted to escape and was killed. The court sentenced Satanta and Big Tree to be hanged. Texas governor Edmund J. Davis commuted both sentences to life imprisonment, and then in 1873 Davis paroled both chiefs. Violating their parole by leading additional raids, Satanta and Big Tree were sent to the Texas penitentiary in Huntsville where Satanta died by falling (or jumping) from a second story window in the prison hospital. Big Tree was later released and became a model citizen on the Kiowa reservation.

One can only imagine what Satanta's fate would have been had he massacred General William Tecumseh Sherman instead of some relatively unknown members of the following party at Salt Creek.

References:

B. W. Aston and Donothan Taylor, *Along the Texas Forts Trail* (Denton: University of North Texas Press, 1997).

W. S. Nye, *Carbine and Lance: The Story of Old Fort Sill* (Norman: University of Oklahoma Press, 1969).

The Saga of Cynthia Ann Parker

The Parker family were normal pioneer settlers living in Parker's Fort in Limestone County, Texas, until the Comanches came on a raid on May 19, 1836. After requesting and being refused a cow, the Indians attacked the fort, killed seven people, and carried off five people including nine-year-old Cynthia Ann Parker. Although the other four captives were subsequently released for ransom, years later Cynthia chose to remain with her captors, and thus she became a primary figure in one of the epic sagas of the American frontier—a saga of romance and ultimate heartbreak.

As a prisoner of the Comanches with no way to return to her own people, Cynthia allowed herself to become assimilated into the Indian way of life. For all practical purposes, she became a Comanche. When seen by a white visitor to her Comanche camp four years after her abduction, Cynthia refused to respond to his questions, and she made no attempt to leave with him.

In her early twenties Cynthia became the wife of Peta Nocona, a prominent Comanche war chief, and she bore him three children. Her first child, Quanah Parker, became famous as the last influential leader of the Comanches. Leading the last

Cynthia Ann Parker
with child Prairie Flower
*Photo courtesy of
Western History Collections,
University of Oklahoma Libraries*

51

of the Comanche bands into Fort Sill in 1875 to go onto a reservation, Quanah Parker brought about the end of hostilities between the Comanches and the whites. He later became Principal Chief of the Comanche Nation, and played a leading role in domesticating tribal members to the white man's civilization.

Loving her husband and her children, Cynthia lived happily among the Comanches until wrenched from that environment in 1860 in the Battle of Mule Creek. The battle occurred as the aftermath of Peta Nocona's last victorious raid on the western edge of Parker County, which ironically was named after Cynthia's family. A family named Sherman was attacked in their home, and the pregnant wife lost her life. Captain Sul Ross and a group of Texas Rangers pursued the Comanches and caught them at a stream named Mule Creek, a tributary of the Pease River.

Taking the Comanches by surprise, the rangers killed and scattered most of the Indians. Overtaking one rider on a horse, Ross was preparing to shoot when the rider held up a small child, and Ross discovered that the rider was a woman. He turned the woman and her child over to Tom Killiheir, who soon identified the woman as Cynthia Ann Parker. Against her will, Cynthia, along with her daughter, Topsannah (Prairie Flower), was sent to resume life with her white relatives. Torn from her husband and her two older children, Cynthia's remaining life was one of heartbreak and despair. Prairie Flower died within three years, and Cynthia died in 1870, ten years after her return home.

There is controversy as to whether Peta Nocona was killed at Mule Creek or whether he was elsewhere at the time and died two years later. Supporting the claim that Nocona died at Mule Creek, Charles Goodnight, a witness to the battle, claimed to have seen and heard Cynthia bending over one of the fallen warriors after the battle and wailing "Nocona" over and over.

Quanah Parker, who was eight years old when his mother was taken, never forgot her. When leading the Comanche band into Fort Sill in 1875, one of his first questions was to inquire if anyone knew anything about his mother. Learning later that she had died, he then set his mind to having her remains brought to Fort Sill. It took years and several letters to the governor of

Texas before permission to move the body was granted. Finally Quanah Parker was allowed to go to Texas where he succeeded in locating his mother's grave. In December 1910 Quanah's son-in-law, Aubra Birdsong, transported the remains of Cynthia and Prairie Flower to Fort Sill, and they were reburied at the nearby Post Oak Mission.

In a memorial service at the mission, Quanah stated that his mother "love Indians so well no want to go back to folks. All same people anyway." He then urged his people to "follow after the white way, get an education, know work, and make a living. Be ready, like my mother, then we all lie together again."

References:

William T. Hagen, *Quanah Parker, Comanche Chief* (Norman: University of Oklahoma Press, 1993).

David G. McComb, *Texas: A Modern History* (Austin: University of Texas Press, 1999).

Tincia Seginski, "Peta Nocona, Father of Quanah Parker Became Principal Chief After His Success at Antelope Hills," *Wild West*, August 1994.

Quanah Parker: A Great Chief and a Good Businessman

Quanah Parker, the great Comanche chief, recognized the "handwriting on the wall." Although never conquered or captured, he foresaw that the Indians must submit to the white man's way of life or suffer extinction. Approaching the gate of Fort Sill, Oklahoma, as the last of the Comanche chiefs to surrender, Parker dismounted and set his horse free, saying, "There goes the spirit of the Comanche."

Successfully making the transition to a different way of life, Quanah Parker learned the English language, became a shrewd businessman, and committed himself to improving the lives of the Comanches. He also retained some of his Indian ways, such as long hair in braids and a family of seven wives and many children. Preferring at first to continue living in tents, Parker finally agreed to move into a large house that cattle baron Burk Burnett built for him in Cache, Oklahoma. On the red roof was a large white star for each of Parker's wives.

Between 1875 and 1911, Parker served as a mediator between the Indians and the white man. Making many visits to Quanah, Texas, which had been named for him, he was always well received.

Quanah Parker, Comanche Chief

Photo courtesy of Western History Collections, University of Oklahoma Libraries

He became a close friend of many influential people including Charles Goodnight, Burk Burnett, and President Theodore Roosevelt.

On one of his visits to Washington, D.C., to negotiate for the Indians, Parker took occasion to show his sense of humor. One government official was doing his best to persuade Parker to give up his polygamous relationships.

"When you get back home, pick out the wife you like best and tell the rest of them they must get out."

Quanah Parker listened silently. Then the official repeated his counsel with increased emphasis.

"Just pick out your favorite wife and tell the others they've got to move."

"You tell 'em," Quanah responded. Quanah knew full well how his wives would react to something like that, and besides, he had no intention of putting any of them out.

Quanah Parker went into the cattle business and became quite wealthy. When the Quanah, Acme, and Pacific Railroad was built in 1903 from Quanah to Floydada, Parker contributed $40,000 to the enterprise. Referring to it as "his" railroad, he took great delight in riding in the engine whenever he pleased and in blowing the whistle and ringing the bells. After each ride, he would proudly announce: "My engine, my railroad."

Quanah Parker was about sixty-six years old when he died of pneumonia and heart failure. In keeping with Comanche custom, a spear-pointed cedar tree was planted at the head of his grave beside that of his mother at Post Oak Cemetery not far from Fort Sill. On his red granite headstone is the following inscription, written by Mrs. Neda Birdsong, one of Parker's daughters:

> Resting here until day breaks
> and Shadows fall, and darkness
> disappears, is
> QUANAH PARKER
> Last Chief of the Comanches

References:

The Medicine Mound Gazette, printed at Quanah, Texas.

Quanah Chamber of Commerce, *Welcome to Hardeman County*.

Herman Lehmann Returns Home After Nine Years with the Comanches

One of the things the Comanches delighted in doing following a raid was carrying off women and children. They were especially delighted whenever capturing white women and children. Probably the most famous such captive was Cynthia Ann Parker, who became the mother of Quanah Parker, the Comanche chief who ended the Comanche conflicts with the whites by submitting his people to life on reservations. Another white captive who deserves mention was Herman Lehmann, a young boy of Germanic stock. Herman's father died when Herman was quite young, and his mother remarried a man named Philip Buchmier. The family moved to a large tract of land in Loyal Valley on the banks of Squaw Creek, about twenty-five miles northwest of Fredericksburg, Texas.

On a spring day in May 1870, Herman's mother sent him, his younger brother, Willie, and their two younger sisters out to scare the birds away from their wheat field. Suddenly, the children found themselves surrounded by a group of Comanches who scooped up the boys and made off with them. Herman was eleven years old, and he was deathly afraid of his captors and their hideously painted faces. Struggling with all his might, Herman almost broke free, but he was subdued and tied by two of the Indians.

Although Willie managed to escape shortly after their capture, Herman spent the next nine years of his life with the Comanches. He not only lived with the Comanches, he essentially became one of them. After a period of time, Herman adapted so completely into the Comanche way of life that he had no desire to leave them.

The process of becoming an Indian had its difficulties as well as occasional humor. On one occasion Herman and a friend, Totoabacona, were out hunting game. Herman was on a mule while his friend rode a swift horse. They encountered a buffalo, which proceeded to charge Herman and his mule. As might be expected, the mule was not in a mood to move. So Totoabacona raced his horse back and forth, staying between the buffalo and the mule. Finally, when the buffalo got too close, Totoabacona shot the beast. But before it died, the buffalo gored the horse and then fell beneath the still stationary mule. The horse ran a short distance and died. Herman jumped from the mule to skin the buffalo, only to find that the animal was not yet dead. Jumping to his feet, the buffalo charged the dismounted Indian, who deftly jumped out of the way, and the buffalo tumbled over a small bluff and died.

Throughout his nine years with the Comanches, Herman's mother never lost faith that her son was still alive. Daily she prayed for his return. Her hopes were strengthened by occasional reports such as one from Adolph Korn, a former captive of the Indians, who reported that he had seen Herman near Fort Sill, Oklahoma, and that he was alive.

Late in 1878 news came that Colonel Ranald S. Mackenzie was traveling from Fort Sill to San Antonio, and that he would be passing near Fredericksburg. Although Mrs. Buchmier was away at the time and missed the colonel as he passed through, she and her husband hurried southward and caught up with Mackenzie before he reached Fredericksburg.

"Yes, there is one white boy there," Mackenzie acknowledged, "but from the description you give, I don't think he is your son."

Herman Lehmann

Photo courtesy of
Western History Collections,
University of Oklahoma Libraries

Reasoning that even if the boy were not her son, it would be good to return him to white people, the colonel agreed to wire Fort Sill and have a detachment of soldiers bring the white boy down to Mrs. Buchmier. Within a few weeks, the boy and the Buchmier family were face to face in Loyal Valley. They did not recognize one another.

It was Willie who finally made the identification. "Mamma, it is Herman. Don't you see the scar on his hand? That is where I cut him with our hatchet." Shouts of praise and thanksgiving to God went out from Herman's mother as she embraced her son with tears of joy. But the twenty-year-old Herman could not respond. After nine years, he had forgotten the English and German he once knew and could only speak the languages of the Comanches.

There was merriment and celebration in the Loyal Valley settlement of 300 persons that evening. But Herman, maintaining typical Indian stoicism, sought every occasion to shun the company of others. He could not eat their food, and he refused to sleep in the feather bed they had prepared for him. When the group of soldiers left for their return trip, Herman tried to go with them, but he was restrained.

For months Willie stayed constantly with Herman until he finally resigned himself to remaining with his birth family. The transition was slow and difficult and was never fully completed. Frequently Herman would throw off his more civilized clothing and don breechcloth and feathers. Sometimes he frightened little children, and sometimes he delighted them with his feats with a bow and arrow. Living in two different worlds at the same time, Herman struggled.

In later years Herman acknowledged the loving attention he received from his family.

"I would try to run away, but Willie would bring me back and the women would cry around me. I did not like tears.

"At last the kindness, tenderness, and gentleness of my good Christian mother, the affectionate love of my sisters, and the vigilance of my brothers gradually wove a net of love around me that is as lasting as time itself."

Although marrying two white women (the first marriage failed), Herman made many visits to Oklahoma to spend time with his Indian friends. He was a white man trying to live in two very different worlds. In his old age, he was living with Willie in Loyal Valley when he died.

References:

A. C. Greene, *The Last Captive* (Austin: The Encino Press, 1972).

Herman Lehmann, *Nine Years with the Indians* (San Antonio: Leheo Graphics, 1985).

Never Bet Against the Comanches in a Horse Race

The Comanches were the best riders on the plains. They were masters of good horsemanship in battle and in hunting. During in-between periods, they enjoyed the sport of horse racing, and when in competition with the whites, they were also good con artists.

At Fort Chadbourne in the late 1800s, a shave-tail lieutenant just out of West Point was bragging about the prowess and speed of his horse and offering to bet that his horse could beat any other horse in Texas in a match race. When the Comanches heard of the lieutenant's boasts, about twenty of them showed up at Fort Chadbourne with a little mustang, shaggy-haired, pitifully thin, and only fourteen hands high. Not being aware that the mustangs, a blend of African, Arabian, and Spanish breeds, were very fast horses, the soldiers thought that their horses could easily beat the little critter standing before them.

Although feeling insulted about racing his sleek cavalry horse against such a nag as the Indian challenger appeared to be, the lieutenant acquiesced to the urging of his comrades and reluctantly accepted the challenge. Bets were placed, with the Indians wagering buffalo robes, buckskins, and turquoise and silver jewelry against the soldiers' silver dollars. The race was run, and the little mustang barely won, outrunning the lieutenant's horse by a neck. Anxious to recoup their losses, the soldiers brought out another horse and challenged the Comanches to another race. Again bets were placed, and this time the mustang barely won by a nose.

The humiliated soldiers then brought out a third horse, a fine Kentucky racing mare, the fastest horse in the fort. They knew that this horse could run faster than the mustang had run in the two previous races. This time the soldiers were betting almost all their personal belongings, and they were going to

60

fleece the Indians at their own game and recover their pride, their honor, and their prior losses. The Kentucky mare was fast. The soldiers failed to notice, however, that after two races, the mustang was not winded.

The race began with the Comanche rider whooping piercingly into his horse's ear, and the mustang jumped to a quick lead. This time the mustang was running at full speed, and as the gap between the two horses widened with every hoof beat, the Kentucky mare was hopelessly outclassed. For the last fifty yards of the quarter-mile race, the Comanche rider sat backwards on his horse shouting taunts to the cursing white rider who was falling farther behind.

After the Indians had left with all their booty, a half-breed interpreter told the dazed soldiers how they had been duped. That Comanche mustang was the fastest horse in all the South Plains and had already won fortunes for its Comanche owners.

Reference:

Jeff Adams, "Comanche Tricksters," *True West*, September-October 1958.

Nelson Lee's Magic Watch Saved His Life

In 1855 just six years after the discovery of gold in California, William Aikens conceived the idea of driving a herd of mules from Texas to California to sell to the miners. "We'll make thousands," Aikens claimed. Agreeing with the proposal, Nelson Lee shouted, "Let's go!"

On a purchasing trip to New Orleans before starting on the westward journey, Lee bought a watch—a large silver watch with an alarm that rang loud and long. With twenty-five hired hands, Lee and Aikens gathered a large herd of mules and started on their journey. Each morning at 3:30, the alarm in Lee's watch announced the start of a new day, and each day's march continued until noon.

All went well on the trail until the early morning of April 3 when the party was about 350 miles northwest of Eagle Pass. Just before 3:30 in the morning Lee awoke to terrifying screams and saw that Comanches were in camp slaughtering and scalping the men. Lee, Aikens, and two others were forced to watch the massacre while four Comanches bound their hands and feet with buffalo thongs. As the slaughter came to an end, one of the Indians picked up Lee's bedroll and found the watch. As the four fascinated Indians examined the timepiece, the 3:30 alarm suddenly sounded, and the startled Indians almost jumped out of their skins. After two minutes the alarm ran down, and the Indians, no longer afraid, wanted Lee to make it sound again.

Thinking that his life might be saved if he could convince the Indians that he was a representative of the Sun God, Lee made peculiar gestures to the sky, and with untied hands he rewound the alarm and set it off again. The four Indians were convinced.

Taking Lee and the three other survivors of the massacre to their chief, the marauding Indians were sure that the Great Spirit would reward them. The chief, Big Wolf, demanded to see the "watch ceremony," whereupon he made Lee a co-resident in his own tent. Lee received favored treatment although forced to experience the additional trauma of witnessing the torture and murder of two of his companions. The Indians guarded Lee and his watch closely, and when Aikens finally managed to escape, Lee became the only surviving hostage. In response to repeated demands of the Indians, Lee repeated the watch ceremony over and over.

Lee continued to sleep in Big Wolf's tent until another Comanche chief, Spotted Leopard, showed up and witnessed the watch ceremony. Equally fascinated, Spotted Leopard bought Lee for the princely sum of 120 horses and three horse-loads of skins. Not as hospitable as Big Wolf had been, Spotted Leopard treated Lee rather cruelly, but as long as Lee could perform the watch ceremony, his life was spared.

Another trade took place when Chief Rolling Thunder learned about Lee. Preferring to pray to the Sun God rather than hunt buffalo, Rolling Thunder bought Lee. Lee became a favorite of Rolling Thunder who even provided a young and pretty squaw to be Lee's wife.

Lee's sojourn with the Comanches continued for three years, although he made several attempts during that time to escape. Every attempt was thwarted, however, until Rolling Thunder became too casual while he and Lee were riding to a powwow of chiefs. While the chief was off his horse and drinking water from a pond, Lee grabbed a tomahawk, split the chief's skull, and dashed away on the chief's horse. After wandering for fifty-six days, Lee finally encountered two Mexican traders who led him to civilization.

Lee's life had been a life of adventure. He had fought in the Blackhawk War, had served in the U.S. and the Texas navies, and had been a Texas Ranger before becoming a horse and mule trader. But after his three-year ordeal as a captive of the Comanches, Lee wanted no more adventure. After recuperating in Texas, Lee retired to his native New York, and he never again ventured out of its quiet solitude. His watch had saved his life, but he had no desire to experience anything else like the trauma and danger of his three years as a captive of the Comanches.

Reference:

Thomas W. Beard Jr., "Comanche Captive," *True West*, May-June 1958.

Dreams Saved Josiah Wilbarger's Life

Josiah Wilbarger won fame by surviving a scalping by Indians. Moving to Texas from Kentucky in 1827, Wilbarger established a farm west of Mina (now Bastrop). At that time he was seventy-five miles from the nearest neighbor, and thus he was an "outside settler." In 1832 another settler, Reuben Hornsby, settled even more remotely south of present-day Austin. It was the custom in those days for travelers to stop with outside settlers for rest and sociability.

In August 1833 Wilbarger and four companions stopped at Hornsby's place while on a surveying trip. After a brief sojourn, they moved on, and about six miles away they were attacked by Comanches. Two of the companions were killed and two escaped, making their way back to the Hornsby home. Wilbarger was left for dead, having been shot in the hip and in the neck and having arrows pierce his legs.

Although he appeared to be dead, Wilbarger was still conscious as an Indian stripped him of his clothing and scalped him. When he was finally left alone, he tried to make his way the six miles back to the Hornsby's but was unable to move very far. Crawling to a pool of water, he drank and then spent the night under a tree, naked and cold. His only item of clothing was a sock, which he placed over his scalped head to protect the wound.

During the night Wilbarger saw his sister, Margaret Clifton, in a dream. She told him to remain under the tree and that he would be rescued. She then disappeared in the direction of the Hornsby house. Wilbarger later learned that Margaret had died in Missouri the day before his dream.

Meanwhile, at the Hornsby home that same night, Mrs. Hornsby also had a dream. Although the two men who escaped the slaughter had reported Wilbarger as one of the dead, Mrs.

Hornsby dreamed of seeing Wilbarger beneath a tree, naked but still alive. Rousing her husband and others, she sent a search party out to look for him. They found him, still under the tree, with the protective sock on his head.

Wilbarger lived eleven more years. Moving to northern Texas, he gave his name to Wilbarger County west of Wichita Falls. Never fully recovering from the scalping, which left his skull diseased, Wilbarger died after accidentally hitting his head on a doorframe.

References:

June Rayfield Welch, *People and Places in the Texas Past* (Dallas: G. L. A. Press, 1974).

Claude Dooley and Betty Dooley, *Why Stop? A Guide to Texas Historical Roadside Markers* (Houston: Gulf Publishing Company, 1985).

The Fredericksburg Easter Fires Commemorate a Treaty

Each year the "Fredericksburg Easter Fires" proclaim the Easter season and also serve as a poignant reminder of a treaty made with the Indians many years ago.

Between October 1845 and April 1846, the Society for the Protection of German Immigrants in Texas sponsored the arrival of over 5,000 immigrants from Germany. From their port of entry at Galveston, the new settlers made their way to New Braunfels in Comal County and then to Gillespie County where they organized the settlement of Fredericksburg. Disease and exposure took their toll, making the first year very difficult for the new community. The Indians constituted another problem by making raids and by shooting arrows at the settlers as they worked in their fields.

Realizing the necessity of peaceful relations, Baron Otfried Hans von Meusebach led a party of forty men to seek peace with the Indians. Riding out to the Comanches' winter encampment in the San Saba country during the Easter season of 1847, Meusebach and his party succeeded in making a treaty with the Comanche chiefs to the effect that the Indians would perpetrate no further hostilities toward the German colonists in exchange for $3,000 worth of presents. From that point in time, the German colonists had less trouble with the Indians than any other group of settlers in Texas, and in later years the Germans took well-deserved pride in their friendly relations with the Indians.

While the negotiations were in progress, the Indians built huge fires on the hilltops around Fredericksburg. These fires, which were first seen the night before Easter Day, would be used as smoke and fire signals in case any treachery toward the Indians became apparent. Peaceful conditions prevailed, however, and the fires were allowed to burn high—high enough that the children in one of the community's families became quite frightened. The mother soothed her children's frightened feelings by telling them that the Easter rabbit had built the fires and was cooking eggs and dying them with colors from the wildflowers that the little rabbits were bringing to her.

When Meusebach and his party returned from their treaty negotiations, they were so intrigued by the story that they vowed to build the fires at Easter each year that the treaty remained in force. The custom continues and has even grown into an annual pageant.

Reference:

"Gillespie County and Fredericksburg, Texas," mimeographed document from the Fredericksburg Information Bureau.

Cattle

Introduction

B eginning with Columbus, the Spanish brought cattle, as well as horses, to the New World. In 1521 they began bringing cattle into Mexico, and wherever missions and forts were established, cattle were provided for food and for labor. It was inevitable that, from time to time, some of these animals would wander from their herds or escape from their enclosures. Grass was plentiful and water was adequate, and for three hundred years, these stray cattle lived, survived, and multiplied in the wild. The various breeds intermixed, and when the Anglos began migrating to Texas in the early 1800s, they found the land filled with splendid multicolored longhorn cattle.

With thin flanks and flat sides, the tough longhorns could forage for themselves, protect themselves from wolves, withstand blizzards and heat, resist ticks and fever, and go for days without water. Although their ratio of meat to bone was rather low, they were numerous, and they were free for the taking.

As the cattle were gathered, the central and western parts of Texas became a land of ranches. Men such as Charles Goodnight became cattle barons overnight, and routes such as the Chisholm Trail were established for moving vast herds to the Kansas railheads for marketing.

Cattle became a major Texas industry, and cattle drives were a major part of that industry. Occasionally rustlers, Indians, and stampedes were problems, but more serious problems arose when farmers started erecting fences that blocked the trails. Open skirmishes between farmers and cattle drovers threatened to erupt into major conflict as each side strove to protect its "rights." The railroads proved to be the ultimate solution as they built into Texas and negated the need for trail drives. Instead of driving the cattle to market, the market came to the cattle.

Joseph McCoy Was the Moving Force Behind the Chisholm Trail

Every age has its entrepreneurs who make things happen and become fabulously rich as a result. Scores of such entrepreneurs arose during America's westward movement, and tales of their exploits are legion. But there are some whose names are relatively unknown, although their accomplishments had far-reaching effects. Joseph McCoy, at the age of twenty-nine, was one such person.

Trail drives from Texas to the northern markets initially followed the Shawnee Trail through Dallas to Preston and then through Indian Territory. Because the longhorn cattle carried ticks that spread Texas fever to other cattle, settlers along the route began objecting to the passage of the longhorns. Some herds were actually turned back at gunpoint. There were also other problems along the route such as unfriendly Indians and bogus tax collectors.

Observing these problems, Joseph McCoy determined in 1867 that an alternate route would be preferable for future trail drives. McCoy talked the Kansas Pacific Railroad into building a branch line from Wyandotte, Kansas, to Abilene, and he agreed to pay the railroad five dollars for every animal shipped over its

Cattle herd on the high plains

Photo courtesy of Western History Collections, University of Oklahoma Libraries

line that year. He then went to Abilene with his two brothers, and they built stockyards capable of holding 1,000 cattle. They also built a barn, an office, a three-story hotel, a large livery stable, and a bank.

As a result of heavy advertising throughout Texas, many cattle barons decided to take a chance on a new route that led to Abilene. Located west of the Shawnee Trail, much of the route had already been blazed. It had plenty of grass, small streams rather than large rivers, and less contention from settlers and Indians. The first trail drive was successful, and the first train, containing twenty cars of cattle, left Abilene for Chicago on September 5, 1867.

One of the early frequent travelers on this new trail was a Cherokee-Scotch trader named Jesse Chisholm. Chisholm had blazed the trail while trading with the Indians, and therefore it was his name that became attached to the new trail.

The famous Chisholm Trail became an important artery from Texas to the cattle markets of the north and east, and it remained in prominence until the advent of refrigerated railroad cars, which made it possible to slaughter the cattle locally and ship the refrigerated meat rather than drive herds over such long distances. Such a refrigerated processing plant was built in 1873 in Denison, Texas, a junction point of the Missouri-Kansas-Texas Railroad. As might be expected, it was this same Joseph McCoy who established that plant.

Reference:

David Morgan, "Life on Chisholm Trail Recreated for Texans," *The Dallas Morning News*, June 24, 1967.

Old Blue was King of the Longhorns

Whenever a group of individuals remain together for a period of time, leaders emerge. This is true of humans, and it is true of animals. Eventually a supreme leader will be acknowledged. Old Blue, a longhorn steer born in South Texas, was such a leader.

In the spring of 1877, the three-year-old Blue was part of a herd of thousands bound for Charles Goodnight's ranch on the Arkansas River just west of present-day Pueblo, Colorado. Each day Blue, with his long, steady stride, made his way to the front of the herd, and he marched between the pointers as they traveled the Goodnight Trail up the valley of the Pecos. Each day the steer's bluish head and tireless legs set the pace for the rest of the herd.

Goodnight quickly recognized that Blue was no ordinary steer, and he retained the animal when the rest of the herd moved on. "Blue, you'll work no more," Goodnight declared. "You'll be the leader of our herd."

Goodnight hung a bell on Old Blue's neck and attached him to a herd bound for Dodge City where they would be loaded into railroad cars bound for the slaughterhouses of Kansas City. The steer seemed to be proud of the clanging of the bell as he walked along with head high and tail swishing. Very quickly, the rest of the herd knew the sound of the bell and accepted it as their clarion call. At night a cowboy would stuff grass into the bell to keep it quiet, but if the grass slipped out, which it occasionally did, the sound of the bell would bring the herd instantly to its feet ready to march.

For eight years Old Blue pointed herds from Texas to Dodge City, sometimes twice a year. Whenever a herd had members who were too frisky or otherwise hard to handle, Old Blue would be sent into the middle, and soon all would be following him and the sound of his bell. In every sense, Old Blue was the leader.

Old Blue won undying fame by saving a Goodnight herd from disaster one winter on the outskirts of Dodge City. The Goodnight cowboys had camped their herd just across the Arkansas River from Dodge City. It was a cold wintry night, and about midnight a severe storm arose, scattering two other herds that were camped nearby. At dawn the situation looked desperate for the Goodnight herd until the trail boss called out, "Loose the bell and take the river." The men saddled up, the grass was removed from the bell's clapper, and with his bell clanging, Old Blue set out for the river. Breaking the ice at the edge of the river, Old Blue swam the stream and headed straight for the railroad corrals with two thousand cattle following. Inside the corral gate he deftly stepped aside as the others crowded in. The cowboys prodded the cattle up the chutes and into the cars, and as the train pulled out, the saddle horses and Old Blue stretched their necks and watched them go.

On occasion Old Blue did other work such as being yoked to outlaw steers who needed to be brought into line. He would drag them to where he wanted them to be, and they learned quickly to conform.

Old Blue—known as the king of the longhorns—spent his last days in retirement on Goodnight's Palo Duro ranch where he was honored and admired. When he finally died of old age, his cowboy friends chopped off his horns and reverently nailed them above the ranch house door.

_____

Reference:

B. A. Botkin, *A Treasury of Western Folklore* (New York: Wings Books, 1975).

Mrs. Robbins Ensures Safe Passage for the Drovers

As a rule, women did not accompany the drovers on the cattle drives to the north. The days were long, the work was hard, and schedules had to be maintained. Although women frequently have greater physical and emotional endurance than men, they were nevertheless considered to be out of place on the trail drives. In addition, there were dangers from Indians, who might be seeking revenge for earlier wrongs or seeking to steal cattle or horses. Many Indian tribes, especially the Comanches, would kidnap women and children whenever the opportunity presented itself and either keep or sell them. Thus, having a woman along on a trail drive was generally considered an invitation to trouble.

Every rule, however, has its exceptions. On a particular drive up the Chisholm Trail, a newlywed man named Robbins brought his bride along for a honeymoon trip. Robbins owned many of the cattle being driven, and despite the objections of the trail boss, Doley Miller, Robbins insisted that his wife's presence would not be detrimental to the progress of the drive. Mrs. Robbins was a beautiful woman, and Miller was sure that some kind of trouble would result, but he finally relented.

All went well until one day when 600 Comanches in full war dress confronted and stopped the drovers. Demanding twenty head of cattle, the Indians appeared intent on obtaining their demands until one of their leaders spotted Mrs. Robbins. Instantly transfixed by her beauty, he rode up to her, leaned down from his horse, and stared eagerly at her for what seemed a long time without moving or speaking. Finally he turned to Mr. Robbins and said, "Me give you five horses for your squaw."

Now any woman who finds herself valued at five horses by an Indian should feel highly flattered. It was an offer not to be refused; nevertheless, Mr. Robbins did refuse it. His hesitation in responding might have been misinterpreted as a consideration of accepting the offer, but in Robbins' mind it was not a question of whether or not to accept the offer, but how to say no in a way that would pacify the Indian and avoid conflict.

Directing Miller to cut out two cows and give them to the Indians, Robbins succeeded in mollifying his wife's Indian suitor. Withdrawing peacefully from the scene, the Comanches gave the drovers unmolested passage through the remaining portions of their territory. Thus instead of being a source of trouble, it was Mrs. Robbins' presence that now guaranteed safe passage for the drovers, all because of one Indian's infatuation with her.

Reference:
The Dallas Morning News, May 17, 1925.

Never Play Tricks on the Chuck Wagon Cook

If asked to name the most important person on a trail drive, most cowboys would agree on the chuck wagon cook. It was the cook's responsibility to keep the men well fed with food fit to be eaten, a task that sometimes required a cook to double as a magician.

Always the first one up each morning, the cook would have a big pot of coffee boiling even before the wrangler got up to round up the saddle horses. Then a typical breakfast of biscuits or flapjacks would be prepared. Before moving out, the crew would agree with the cook on the camp location for the next night, and it was up to the cook to get his wagon, pulled by four ornery mules, to that location as best he could. After cleaning pots and pans and loading all the bedrolls and other things left by the crew, the cook would start on his own journey to the specified location.

Those mules took the chuck wagon across open country between boulders, stumps, and trees; across streams; up and down hills. The cook had to get there no matter what and have a good, hearty meal ready for the hungry crew when they arrived with their cattle. That was his job, and the gang didn't care how he did it as long as he got it done.

Cowboys seated around a chuck wagon

Photo courtesy of Western History Collections, University of Oklahoma Libraries

The evening meal was usually set out in the pots in which it was cooked. There would be a big pot of soup, another pot of roast beef with every kind of vegetable in it, a pot of beans, a pot of sourdough biscuits. The cowboys would simply help themselves.

A rapport always existed between a good cook and the others in the crew, and they frequently took time to chat, trade yarns, and even play tricks on each other. It was smart to be well liked by the cook, even though friendly shenanigans would sometimes take place.

One chuck wagon cook recalled in later years how the men in his crew, who had played several tricks on him, expressed their distaste for bear meat. Bear meat is coarse-grained with a strong "gamey" flavor, but when well cooked, it can be just as palatable as buffalo, venison, or elk meat. To the men of this crew, the carcass of a skinned bear looked too much like a human carcass, and they wanted no part of it.

This particular cook saw an opportunity to play a trick on the men who had played many tricks on him. Knowing that a good friend who was homesteading in the area had recently killed a bear, the cook also knew that he would soon be driving by that homestead. Stopping in for a brief visit, the cook obtained a whole hindquarter of the bear. Using two Dutch ovens that afternoon, he cooked venison in one and bear meat in the other. Then, instead of leaving the meats in their pots, he piled both meats high on the same platter and served them for supper. Not knowing what they were eating, the cowboys thought all the meat was delicious. It was not until they all sat around the campfire that night that the mischievous cook told them what they had eaten. The cowboys ranted and raved and threatened the cook with mayhem, but the scales of justice were somewhat evened. They kept eating whatever the cook served, and they continued having a good time with one another.

Reference:

Mark Trey, "Chuck Wagon Chuckles," *True West*, September-October 1958.

The Fence Cutters Fight for Survival

It can be safely claimed that barbed wire transformed the West as much as any other influence. Not only did fences block roads and trails, they also isolated springs and ponds from thirsty cattle. Thus, the Indians were not the only ones who did not like fences. To ranchers whose cattle grazed the open range and who drove their cattle to the northern markets, barbed wire was a tool of the devil that threatened their very existence. The situation became one of land ownership versus the open range, and it became quite volatile. It also led to a new category of frontiersmen—that of "fence cutters."

The terrible drought of 1883 was especially hard on the cattle of Texas. Thirsty and emaciated cattle were dying by the hundreds. With little enough water anyway on the parched and cracked land, the fact that many water sources were fenced off and unavailable to the cattle made fence cutting a necessity.

Organizing themselves loosely but secretively, fence cutters would frequently stay out late at night and then come home without letting their wives know where they had been or what they had been doing. Such excursions resulted in a few less fences than before. Occasionally there was bloodshed along with the fence cutting, but the fence cutters usually tried intimidation first.

A Castroville farmer woke up one morning to find a card with a bullet hole in it attached to one of his fences. The card read, "If you don't make gates, we will make them for you."

After cutting a fence in Live Oak County, the fence cutters dug a grave and dangled a rope in it. The note they left read, "This will be your end if you rebuild this fence."

Repairing a fence in Coleman County that had previously been cut, a sheep man found a coffin on his front porch. The attached note said, "This is what you will need if you keep fencing." The resourceful sheep man was not easily intimidated, however, and he used the coffin as a watering trough.

Some of the fence builders were sympathetic to the needs of the cattle, especially during the 1883 drought. At Gonzales, Doc Burnet found some of his neighbors' cattle standing at the gate of his pasture looking longingly at the water within. Opening the gate, he invited them in, and then he invited his neighbors to use his water at any time. He also offered to pull up his fencing until the drought ended. Burnet never had any trouble with fence cutters.

Men like Doc Burnet were the exception, however, and tensions continued to mount. Many fence cutters employed armed guards to protect them while they cut. In defense, landowners began placing sticks of dynamite along their fences. Finally, in an attempt to diffuse the situation, the Texas Legislature made fence cutting a felony. At the same time they made it illegal to erect fencing on public lands or around land belonging to another. The invention of refrigerated railroad cars further diffused the situation by enabling cattle to be slaughtered locally and their carcasses shipped to market.

In the end, the West was transformed. Although large ranches did and still do exist, land ownership and fencing brought permanent change.

Reference:

Wayne Gard, *Frontier Justice* (Norman: University of Oklahoma Press, 1949).

Civil War

Introduction

With its vastness and its plentiful and varied resources and natural environments, Texas belonged to two different worlds. It was truly a part of the great Southwest with its semi-arid plains, its cattle, its cowboys and Indians, and its remote openness that served as havens for lawless adventurers.

On the other hand, Texas was a southern state, allied in most respects with the other states of the Deep South. Texas, especially in its central and eastern portions, had vast cotton plantations with slaves providing the necessary labor. Thus, a southern aristocracy arose similar to that in the Southeast.

When the South seceded from the Union, Texas seceded also, although against the advice of Governor Sam Houston. As one of the Confederate States of America, Texas participated in the Civil War, and Texans raised many fighting units for defense at home and for action in other parts of the South.

It should be noted, however, that Texas had its share of Northern sympathizers. Populated by colonists from the North who opposed secession as well as by colonists from the South who favored secession, Texas became a land of internal conflict. Although there were occasional open hostilities between the two factions, the Southern sympathizers who were in the greater majority predominated and maintained a relatively peaceful climate.

Following the Civil War, Reconstruction brought political and economic turmoil to Texas as well as to the other southern states, and there were various local conflicts between the southern residents and the Yankee "do-gooders" for many more years.

Dr. Gideon Lincecum Expresses His Feelings Toward the North

With the Civil War now a 140-year-old memory, it is difficult for persons living today to grasp the intensity and depth of anti-Northern feelings that pervaded the South during that tragic period of American history. Southern agrarianism supported a proud and wealthy aristocracy in a manner that would be impossible without that "relic of barbarism," slavery. To southerners, the "do-gooders" and hypocrites in the North were intent on destroying not only slavery but an entire way of life. Therefore, this was a war of survival against a hated Northern regime that had no business interfering in the first place.

In letters written to relatives and friends in the 1860s, Dr. Gideon Lincecum, a plantation owner in Washington County, Texas, expressed his intense feelings about the events then taking place. The vehemence of his feelings may be surprising or even repugnant to the reader, but they give a quite accurate representation of the spirit and drive that motivated Southern secession and the formation of the Confederacy.

In a letter dated December 3, 1860, Dr. Lincecum expressed the optimism that pervaded the South as secession and war loomed imminent.

We are very capable of sustaining an independent government, and with our very abundant rich resources, a very wealthy one. We know the value of our cotton and sugar will engage the attention, and if we require it, the assistance of foreign powers; and we'll call them most certainly, before we will agree to yield our necks to the yoke that has been prepared for us by Northern fanaticism.

In the same letter, Dr. Lincecum speaks of the high level of excitement, the mass meetings, conventions, and militiamen in readiness. "Lone Star flags and blue cockades are fluttering to every breeze and glittering on every hat, as well as on the breast of many of our patriotic ladies." Lincecum expressed the desire that there not be any fighting, but "we intend to withdraw from the federal Union, and we are organizing, arming, and equipping ourselves for the purpose of sustaining our republic in a style that will deter invasion."

Never hesitating to state his own feelings, Dr. Lincecum in another letter wrote: "I am out and out a secessionist, which must suffice for me on the subject of politics."

Interwoven with the Southern optimism was the anger and bitterness with which southerners in general regarded the North. Again, Dr. Lincecum speaks for the South as well as for himself.

> If the North should hold on to the fool notion that she can coerce the cotton states into submission to her despotic plans, and undertakes a war with us, she will be brought to bed with a most disastrous disappointment. For we won't be satisfied with thrashing them, but it will then, be their turn to submit to such terms as the exasperated southern confederacy may think proper to grant them.

Texas did not experience the fullness of privations and suffering experienced in the Deep South, and although things were not going well for the South in 1865, Lincecum's hatred of the North was only intensified. His former optimism, however, does not show in his later letters. On January 27, 1865, Lincecum wrote:

> We are all healthy, and ready to put up with anything that can befall us, except subjugation to Yankee rule. Death, in any form, Satan or any imp of the infernal regions to rule over us in preference to any Yankee arrangement.

Upon receiving news of Abraham Lincoln's assassination, Lincecum vented his views in support of the assassin. To Americans today who view Lincoln as one of the greatest of American leaders, Lincecum's views may seem shocking, but in those days, southerners viewed Lincoln as almost the Antichrist.

> *I see by the papers that came today, that the story of this killing of the cold hearted tyrant Lincoln is no joke. I hope the man who performed that great piece of public service to the nations, may make good his escape, and that he may live to burst the skulls of a few more of the despots.*

Lee's surrender to Grant at Appomattox was a hard thing for southerners to accept. According to William Abernathy, of McKinney, Texas, who was present at Appomattox: "No man can ever describe what followed. Some sat at the roots of trees and cried as if their hearts would break. Some grasped the Winfield rifles that they had carried for years and smashed them. Some cursed bitterly; some prayed."

As one who never fully accepted the Confederate defeat, Lincecum migrated to Tuxpan, Mexico, in 1868 where he joined a colony of former Confederates. He died in 1874 in Texas on a visit to his old home in Washington County.

Reference:

Jerry Bryan Lincecum and Edward Hake Phillips, "Civil War Letters of Dr. Gideon Lincecum," *Texas Studies Annual*, 1955.

Some Texas Slaves Had Good Lives, Some Didn't

Texas really belongs to two quite different sections of America. As a part of the Southwest, Texas had the expected elements: cattle, cowboys, Indians, and arid expanses. In the minds of many people, the Southwest extends the width of Texas to the Louisiana border. But Texas is also a part of the Southeast. Most of the Anglo population of Texas came from the Southeast. Texas sided with the South against the North and joined the Confederacy. Cotton plantations and slavery, hallmarks of the southern economy, were also found in Texas. Actually, the topography and culture of Texas is roughly divided by a north-south line by which the western part of the state has a Southwest flavor and the eastern part has a Southeast flavor. Cotton plantations abounded in southeast Texas. (The mansions of five former plantations along the Brazos River are currently tourist attractions.)

Although much has been written about the harshness of slavery, many plantation owners did their best to provide a measure of enjoyment and humane treatment. Many plantation owners took good care of their slaves, feeding them well, not requiring them to work in inclement weather, caring for their health, and providing a measure of recreation.

One emancipated slave mused in retrospect, "Life on the old plantation was pretty good." From another freed slave, "If old Missy Cunningham ain't in heaven right now, then there isn't any, 'cause she was so good to us we all loved her." From a third, "Me and my young master had good times. He was near my age, and we'd steal chickens from old miss and go down in the orchard and barbecue them. One time she caught us and sure wore us out."

One of the more enjoyable activities for the slaves was the corn shucking sessions in the fall. Along with the work, there could be much laughing, joking, and singing. Slaves from several plantations were sometimes allowed to get together on a single shucking activity. The planter provided the corn along with food and whiskey. As they shucked, the men would hope to find a red ear of corn as that entitled the lucky one to kiss any woman of his choice. The girls as well as the men liked this aspect of the work. After the work a fire would be built, and with music made by scratching on skillet lids, beating bones together, or plucking on homemade banjos and fiddles, the slaves would dance, sometimes until dawn.

Those slaves fortunate enough to belong to benevolent masters had a relatively good life. According to Abraham Sells, a former slave, "You see, we all had pretty good times on Massa Rimes' plantation. None of them cared about being set free. They had to work hard all the time, but that didn't mean so much, 'cause they had to work if they were on their own too."

Life on other plantations was not so pleasant. The slaves worked hard, and the days were long. Weeding, hoeing, planting, picking, and general maintenance were normal daytime activities. Beatings were frequent punishment for slaves whose work was not up to expectations. Although this practice could be quite inhumane, it sometimes led to interesting circumstances.

One young slave girl, after being beaten, went into hiding in the woods. To feed herself she would sneak back to the "big house" and steal fresh-baked bread cooling on the windowsill. Although the master and his dogs failed to find her, she nevertheless came back to her family after a few days. When asked how she evaded the dogs, she explained, "I put pepper in my stockings and ran without shoes. The dogs would sniff the pepper and start sneezing, and they wouldn't follow me."

On some plantations the owner or the overseer administered beatings. Other owners would hire professional beaters. Beatings were frequent on Marse Tom's plantation. On one occasion he hired five men to come and administer beatings. While awaiting their arrival, Sam and Billie, two of the biggest slaves on the place, managed to get shotguns out of the big house. When the five men arrived, Marse Tom was in a rocker on the porch, with Sam and Billie standing by him with their guns. As the men approached, Sam told Marse Tom, "First white man who sets himself inside that fence gets it from the gun." Waving the men back, Marse Tom called out, "Stay outside gentlemen, please do. I've changed my mind." After a further exchange of words, the men reminded Tom that he had hired them, but if he would pay them three dollars apiece, they would leave. William Moore, a former slave, related the story without mentioning any punishment to Sam and Billie.

References:

Ronnie C. Tyler and Lawrence R. Murphy, *The Slave Narratives of Texas* (Austin: The Encino Press, 1974).

Elizabeth Silverthorne, *Plantation Life in Texas* (College Station: Texas A&M University Press, 1986).

Dick Dowling Defeats the Union at Sabine Pass

In the southeast corner of Texas, the Sabine River, which constitutes the border between Texas and Louisiana, empties into a large lake that in turn empties through Sabine Pass into the Gulf of Mexico. During the Civil War, Sabine Pass was a major port through which the southern states sent their cotton to Europe and through which they imported arms and munitions. Thus Sabine Pass had great strategic importance. It was important to the South to keep it open, and it was equally important to the North to have it closed.

Near the mouth of Sabine Pass the South had established Fort Griffin, a small earthwork post with six cannon, to fend off Northern attempts to block the outlet to the Gulf. The fort was garrisoned by the Davis Guards, a group of forty-two Irishmen from nearby Houston, under the command of a twenty-year-old lieutenant named Richard (Dick) Dowling. A narrow dirt road connected the fort to the nearby community of Sabine Pass, and Kate Dorman, owner of the Catfish Hotel in Sabine Pass, used the road to keep Dowling's troops supplied with food.

Dick Dowling: hero of Sabine Pass

Photo courtesy of
G. U. Hubbard Collection

Late in the evening of September 6, 1863, Dowling observed the signal lights of a Union invasion force approaching in the Gulf. Just a few weeks earlier two Union gunboats had succeeded in blockading the pass but were driven away by two Confederate ships sent from Houston. It now appeared that the Union was going to try again.

Dowling immediately awakened his men and ordered them to get ready. "Wake up, boys," he cried.

"There's something brewing, and we had better go to work." The men cleaned their guns, they piled powder and balls, and the fort's engineer went from gun to gun, making sure they were ready. The doctor prepared himself with a supply of splints and bandages. Then they waited.

As the sun rose, nothing had happened. Somewhat disappointed about losing sleep and having to work all night for nothing, the defenders did some scowling and muttering. Dowling consoled them and got them back on track by telling them, "Never mind, boys. Never mind. There is surely something brewing, and let us prepare for whatever may come."

And come, it did. That evening the masts of the invading fleet came into view. Four gunboats, twenty-two troop ships, and fifteen thousand soldiers were approaching. Trouble was surely brewing for Dick Dowling and his forty-two Irish defenders from Houston.

Captain Frederick Odlum, in the village of Sabine Pass, sent word to General John Bankhead Magruder in Houston. In response, Magruder suggested that it was an impossible situation, and that Fort Griffin should be abandoned, but he left the final decision up to Odlum and Dowling. At the fort, Dowling assembled his men and asked their opinion. "What do you say, men? Shall we retreat, or shall we stay and fight it out?"

"No, no, no!" they shouted back. "Fight, fight, fight!"

"Then to your guns," cried Dowling. "See that everything is ready. But don't fire until I give the signal."

Into the night the ships approached nearer and nearer, and at daybreak (September 8) the Union gunboats began firing on the fort and on the road connecting the fort to the village. Dowling restrained his men from returning fire. "Not yet, boys. They are too far off, and we haven't a ball or a pound of powder to throw away."

The slow and steady Union approach continued, and the pounding of the fort and road continued. Then at three o'clock in the afternoon, when the ships were close enough for the voices of the Union soldiers and sailors to be heard, Dowling fired his cannon.

"Load and fire at will!" he shouted. With that as the signal, the other Confederate guns roared into action.

Masts were ripped off the leading ships. A loud explosion sent one ship, the *Sachem*, into the air as a ball exploded her boilers. Another ship, the *Clifton*, raised the white flag after a severe pounding. A third ship, the *Arizona*, was wounded and backed away out of cannonball range. She was so damaged that her crew threw horses, provisions, and everything else they could overboard to lighten her weight. The remaining ships turned and left the scene of action.

As the battle ended, Dowling and his men had captured two Union gunboats and crippled a third. They took 350 prisoners, thirteen cannon, and much ammunition and provi-

Dick Dowling monument
at Sabine Pass

Photo courtesy of
G. U. Hubbard Collection

sions. Among the prisoners was Lieutenant Frederick Crocker of the *Clifton*, who asked to see the Confederate commander. He could hardly believe his eyes as Dick Dowling, a young, dirty, twenty-year-old boy presented himself. Crocker was even more amazed when he saw the mere handful of Texas Irishmen who had beaten the large armada. "Four gunboats and fifteen thousand men beaten by this boy and his forty-two Irishmen," he muttered. "It is something unheard of."

It truly was an accomplishment, and the young Dowling and his men had achieved one of the South's greatest victories.

Reference:

E. G. Littlejon, *Texas History Stories* (Richmond: B. F. Johnson Publishing Co., 1901).

Prisoners of War Must Try to Escape

When Union soldiers imprisoned at Camp Ford in Tyler, Texas, learned of a successful escape from Libby Prison in Richmond, Virginia, thoughts of a similar action became ingrained in their thoughts. If the Union prisoners at Libby Prison could tunnel their way out of their prison camp, so could the prisoners at Camp Ford.

In a covered dugout near the deadline (the outer limits of the area freely available to the prisoners), a small group of prisoners started digging. Working at night, only one person at a time could be in the narrow tunnel, and the other members of the group stationed themselves in the dugout ready to pack the removed dirt onto the roofs of the nearby dugouts. Initially the digger used a spade stolen from the prison guards, but in the narrowness of the tunnel, the spade proved unwieldy. The diggers then resorted to using a butcher knife to cut through the sticky red East Texas clay, stacking about a cubic foot of soil at a time on a wooden sled. Then pulling the sled out, other men distributed the soil inconspicuously in the darkness. The tunnel was so confining that each digger had to be replaced after two or three sled loads.

The work proceeded very slowly, and after two months the prisoners were on the verge of giving it up. But then they realized that they had gone far enough and now they had only to dig upward. In all that time they succeeded in keeping their project a secret from the Confederates. On one occasion when rumors of the escape tunnel reached Confederate ears, a search was made of the various dugouts. In the hut where the tunnel opening was located, all the Confederate guards saw was a "sick" prisoner stretched out on the floor so as to conceal the tunnel opening.

Finally, on the night of September 27, 1864, the escape attempt commenced. Some thirty-five prisoners organized themselves into squads of three to five persons, and one at a time they squeezed themselves through the tunnel between guard rounds. Everything proceeded successfully until an unusually large man in the last squad became wedged in the tunnel. Panicking, he sounded the alarm by crying out for help. Hard riding rangers and guard dogs sprang into action and recaptured all but two of the escaped squads.

Throughout the Civil War, prisoners on both sides used a wide variety of methods and daring in attempting to escape their confinements. Although most attempts failed, some were successful and others were partially successful, such as the escapade cited above. Patient hard work led to success in some of the escape attempts, while other attempts succeeded primarily because of daring on the parts of the captives and ineptitude on the parts of the captors.

Consider the case of Union Private Horace B. Little, who borrowed a nurse's pass from one of the male nurses at the Camp Ford hospital and forged a copy for himself and two friends. At the gate leading out of the prisoners' compound, a guard examining their pass said that it was not countersigned by the commandant. When Little insisted that the signature was really there but couldn't be seen in the dark, the guard took his word for it and allowed the three prisoners to pass through the gate, presumably on their way to render service at the hospital. Then, as luck would have it, they encountered the commandant himself outside the compound fence. Striding toward the hospital with looks of determination as though on an important mission, the prisoners saluted the commandant and passed him without being challenged.

Knowing how conspicuous they would be at the hospital with no official duties to perform, the escapees wondered what they should do next. Fortunately, the nurse whose pass they had copied, met them and gave them sacks, suggesting they go into the woods and pick grapes. That night as the three prisoners hid in the woods, their nurse friend brought them some food. Crawling through the woods to escape detection by pickets posted throughout the area, Little and one of his companions made their way out of the area, although the third person, suffering from cut and infected feet, had to be left behind.

Traveling northward, Little and his remaining companion eventually reached Union lines.

Reference:

Robert G. Glover, *Camp Ford: Tyler Texas, C. S. A.* (Nacogdoches: East Texas Historical Association, 1998).

Northern and Southern Sympathies Clashed in Cooke County

On February 28, 1861, the people of Texas went to the polls and voted by a three to one margin for secession. But in north-central Texas, the vote in Cooke County, along with that of twenty-one other Texas counties, favored remaining in the Union. Although Cooke County and its county seat, Gainesville, had more settlers from southern states than from northern states, the majority of its southern settlers were not slaveholders, and they had no desire to fight for someone else's slaves. On the other hand, the Southern sympathizers included some of Cooke County's leading citizens. The county's two large plantation owners, James Bourland and William C. Young, who were leaders in the events pertaining to the Great Hanging, were also colonels in the Confederate militia detachments stationed in the Gainesville area.

Ever since the John Brown escapade in 1859, tensions were running high throughout the South, and with secession now taking place, those tensions reached boiling points in those areas where sympathies were more or less equally divided. In Cooke County, the tensions boiled over with tragic results.

The Confederate Conscription Act of April 16, 1862, which required military service from all southern males between the ages of eighteen and thirty-five, brought a storm of protest from Northern sympathizers in Cooke County. Because slaveholders who owned ten or more slaves were exempt from military service, many non-slaveholders became adamant in their opposition to having to fight "for another man's slaves." Not being able to sway the issue, however, the Northern sympathizers went underground. Organizing a secret fraternal order known as the Union League (also called the Peace Party), they created secret rituals, handshakes, and passwords. Pledged to resist all Confederate laws, the Union League also laid plans for assisting an expected invasion by Union troops.

The Union League operated without detection until one September evening in 1862 when an inebriated Ephraim Childs spilled the beans to a local mail carrier, J. B. McCurley, during a drinking session in one of Gainesville's saloons. McCurley informed the Confederate military authorities and then accepted the assignment of infiltrating the Union League and finding out more of their plans. Riding out to the ranch of Dr. Henry Childs, Ephraim's brother, McCurley made inquiries about some supposedly lost livestock and worked his way into Henry's confidence in the process. Before the day was over, McCurley had been sworn into the Union League, had learned its handshake and password, and had learned about the expected Union invasion of Texas. He also learned of Unionists' plans to strike against the secessionists on the night of October 1. Not wishing to be more involved in the matter, McCurley withdrew from his investigative activities, and the local authorities then sent Newton Chance to ferret out more information, which he did with further success.

The strike, if indeed there was to be one, did not materialize, possibly because of a torrential downpour that occurred the night of October 1. Nevertheless, Colonel Bourland dispatched squads of armed riflemen throughout the county, and shortly after dawn, wholesale arrests were made of anyone and everyone suspected of being a Northern sympathizer. While most of the Unionists surrendered peacefully, two of them managed to escape to Arkansas, leaving their families behind. That night the terrified citizens of Gainesville who had not been arrested stayed home behind locked doors.

The next day a "citizens court" convened with a jury containing seven slaveholders to begin a series of trials, the outcome of which could hardly be in doubt. First, Henry Childs was tried and sentenced to death by hanging which occurred two days later on October 4. In an open wagon driven by a slave named Bob Scott, Henry was driven down California Street to the east bank of Pecan Creek where a giant elm tree stretched out over the stream. With Henry still sitting in the wagon, the executioners placed a noose around his neck and then drove the wagon out from under him. Next, Henry's brother, Ephraim, met the same fate. A total of seven men were thus tried and hanged.

A mob then formed and demanded that the jury release all remaining prisoners for hanging. Effecting a compromise agreement, the jury released fourteen men who were promptly lynched by the mob. As of October 13, a total of twenty-three victims could be counted. This might have been the end of the matter had not further trouble ensued.

On October 16 a prominent cotton planter named James Dickson was shot and killed from ambush, and Colonel Young was shot and killed while leading a search for the snipers. Blame immediately fell upon members of the Union League, and the following Sunday the mob demanded the hanging of all remaining prisoners. Again the jury compromised, and they released another nineteen Unionist prisoners, who had been scheduled to be freed, to the frenzied mob. These nineteen were marched to the hanging tree where they also were lynched.

Commemorative monument at Gainesville's
Georgia Davis Bass Park, site of the Great Hanging
Photo courtesy of G. U. Hubbard Collection

At least seven more deaths occurred before these tragic events subsided. Jim Young, the Colonel's son, tracked down one man suspected of killing his father and brought him back to Cooke County where he hanged him in the presence of Young's slaves. Young then went to Sherman in Grayson County and sought out the pro-Union editor of the *Sherman Patriot*, who had praised Colonel Young's murderer. Young shot and killed the editor on the steps of his newspaper office.

Tensions ran high outside of Cooke County as well. For example, in nearby Decatur, five Union League members suspected of conspiracy and treason were hanged.

The "Great Hanging at Gainesville" was a tragic chapter in the course of a tragic Civil War.

References:

David Paul Smith, "Frontier Defense in Texas, 1861-1865" (Denton: North Texas State University Ph.D. Dissertation, 1987).

Michael Collins, *Cooke County, Texas: Where the South and the West Meet* (Gainesville: Cooke County Heritage Society, 1998).

Collin County Feels the Civil War

The Civil War was devastating in a number of ways. In addition to the terrible loss of life on the battlefields, the requirement that every able-bodied man enlist in the army left many farming families in dire circumstances. The women and children left behind while the men were away at war had extreme difficulties maintaining their homes and farms by themselves, and many were incapable of the intensive labor required. Those fortunate enough to own slaves had things a little easier. The experiences of some of the settlers of Collin County, Texas, typify the general effects of the Civil War on the home front.

As was the practice throughout the South, Collin County deserters were hunted down, arrested, and imprisoned. At times it was a heart-wrenching process. Robert C. Horn, a minister in Collin County who helped track down deserters in that area, recalled, "This was a hard business—to take a man away from his home while his wife and children begged and screamed for his release."

In one extreme case, a soldier named McDurmitt, while stationed in Indian Territory (now Oklahoma), received a plaintive letter from his wife. Writing of the hardships the family was enduring in Collin County, she lamented that there was no water within several miles and she had no way of getting her children to water or food. With letter in hand, McDurmitt went to his commanding officer and requested a leave of absence. Upon being refused, he went home without leave and moved his family to where water was available. After spending a short period helping out at home, McDurmitt reported back for duty, whereupon he was immediately arrested. Following a court-martial, McDurmitt was shot as a deserter.

While desertion was treated with utmost severity, the appearance of patriotism and desire to serve drew compassionate reactions in many cases. Many teenage boys who tried to enlist were rejected because of their age. In relatively rare cases, young adults who were considered to be essential at home were similarly rejected from military service. In 1861 Elbert W. Kirkpatrick attempted to enlist in the Confederate army, but he was rejected because he was only seventeen years of age and because he was needed at home. Elbert had been the sole support of his family since his father's death in the 1850s from pneumonia contracted while trying to catch an alligator in a Collin County stream. Reapplying every year, the young Kirkpatrick was finally accepted into the army in 1864, and he participated in several battles.

Lee's surrender to Grant at Appomattox had a heartbreaking impact throughout the South, and tears of frustration and regret were shed by even the hardest of souls. Passions in Collin County were just as strong as those throughout the South. For many years Collin County veterans of the "lost cause" gathered for an annual reunion at Elbert Kirkpatrick's home to remember their more glorious years.

Reference:

Julia L. Vargo, *McKinney, Texas: The First 150 Years* (Virginia Beach: The Donning Company, 1997).

The Jaybirds Oust the Woodpeckers in Fort Bend County

As was the general case throughout the South, the Civil War died slowly in Fort Bend County, Texas. In 1888 the two political factions in Fort Bend were the Jaybirds and the Woodpeckers. The Jaybirds, made up of wealthy residents and "regular democrats" still dedicated to the Southern cause, bitterly opposed the Northern sympathizers who were organized as the Woodpeckers.

As the election of 1888 approached, the animosity between the two parties erupted in armed conflict in which J. M. Shamblin, the Jaybird leader, was killed and others were

Jaybird monument at
Richmond, Texas
Photo courtesy of
G. U. Hubbard Collection

wounded. Certain members of the Woodpeckers were given ten hours to leave town, which they wisely did. A contingent of Texas Rangers arrived to keep the peace on election day, and heavy voting gave control of the county to the Woodpeckers.

The Jaybirds' dissatisfaction with the election results smoldered and finally led to further conflict on August 16, 1889, when the two parties fought the "Battle of Richmond."

After twenty minutes of open warfare and five deaths, the Woodpeckers retreated into the courthouse at Richmond where they surrendered to Texas governor Sul Ross, who had arrived to take command of the situation. The end result was the resignation or removal of all Woodpeckers from public offices in the county.

Adjacent to the City Hall in Richmond, a tall monument with a Jaybird on top has been erected as a memorial to the cause of freedom and in remembrance of three Jaybirds who lost their lives in the several skirmishes with the Woodpeckers. Bearing the following inscription, the monument serves as a fitting reminder of a Richmond version of a Confederate victory.

H. H. Frost
L. E. Gibson
J. M. Shamblin

These brave and noble sons of Fort Bend County,
whose names are here enshrined, gave their lives in order that
the people of this county might have a just,
honest, and capable county government, and their
fellow citizens have reared this monument to their
memory and as a promise to them that their principles
shall be maintained for all time to come.

Go stranger and to the Jaybirds tell that for their
country's freedom they fell.

Reference:

Ann Ruff, *Amazing Texas Monuments & Museums* (Houston: Lone Star Books, 1984).

Law and Order

Introduction

Frontier Texas was liberally blessed with "good guys" who sought to preserve law and order and "bad guys" who seemed as happy to shoot as to eat. Throughout the entire American westward movement, the gunslingers on both sides of the law are legendary, and tales of daring and heroism abound.

In the absence of soldiers or regularly established civil peacekeeping organizations, the early Texas colonies had to employ their own law enforcement bodies to act in their behalf. Protection was needed from Indian and Mexican raiders. Although there was no central authority in those early days, these bodies were commonly referred to as rangers because of their practice of pursuing fleeing raiders wherever they went. These ranger bodies originated in Stephen F. Austin's colony in 1823, and the concept quickly spread to other colonies in Texas.

The initial mission of these rangers was two-fold: to protect the colonists against Indian attacks and to secure the nebulous Mexican border against incursions of Mexican bandits and troops. In their campaigns to quell marauding Mexicans, the rangers sometimes fought alone and sometimes fought alongside or as part of the Texas army before statehood and the U.S. Army after statehood. They were available, they were mobile, and they were effective.

Once the Indian and Mexican dangers were overcome, the rangers turned their attentions to the outlaws, and they went wherever needed to maintain law and order. Gradually the various bodies of rangers became molded into an overall organization, and in 1870 the term "Texas Ranger" came into being through a legislative enactment. The Texas Rangers have continued to be a unique law enforcement agency called upon whenever local authority was absent or needed to be augmented.

The "bad guys" maintained prominent visibility during Texas's formative years. Local sheriffs dealt with them as best they could, some more effectively than others, and the Texas Rangers answered many calls for assistance. Although ready to shoot at a moment's notice, many outlaws claimed to have killed only in self-defense, and many escaped prosecution.

In more than one case, some gunslingers were simply where the action was, sometimes on one side of the law and sometimes on the other. John Wesley Hardin, for example, spent part of his career practicing law, and Ben Thompson, also a prolific killer, ultimately became a sheriff at Austin.

Captain Bill McDonald Begins His Law Enforcement Career

William Jesse McDonald became probably the most well known and most respected of any of the Texas Rangers. On innumerable occasions, Captain Bill, as he was more familiarly known, faced death displaying a calm confidence and fearlessness. Often outnumbered by the subjects he intended to arrest, Captain Bill nevertheless prevailed. It was once said that McDonald would "charge hell with a bucket of water."

With nerves of steel, McDonald served twenty years as a Texas Ranger, and he kept his speed and reflexes sharply tuned. Avoiding tobacco and stimulants of any kind, including tea and coffee, he once explained, "Sometimes I have to be about two-fifths of a second quicker than the other fellow, and a little quiver, then, might be fatal."

McDonald's legendary law enforcement career began in Mineola, Texas, when a mean pit bull dog bit and injured McDonald's prized pointer. The dog belonged to George Gordon, who was just as mean as the dog. Gordon, large and ugly, always carried a pistol and a Bowie knife, and he was reputed to have already killed several persons. McDonald also had a reputation as a man not to mess with. Pulling out his six-shooter with every intent of killing the pit bull, McDonald was clearly in charge of the situation. Gordon pled for mercy, promising to keep his animal at home in the future, and McDonald let them go.

In order to be duly authorized to deal with Gordon in the future, should the need arise, McDonald applied to become a deputy sheriff in Mineola, and he was immediately sworn in. Thus began Captain Bill McDonald's first stint as an official law enforcement officer.

Bill McDonald,
Texas Ranger Captain

*Photo courtesy of
Western History Collections,
University of Oklahoma Libraries*

As fate would have it, McDonald was soon called upon to deal with Gordon and his meanness again. On a drunken spree one night, Gordon was brandishing his weapons in a saloon and generally terrorizing the entire clientele while proclaiming that no one could stop him or arrest him. McDonald showed up very suddenly, and with lightning fast moves, he disarmed Gordon and marched him off to jail. Gordon ranted and raved loudly through the night and into the next day until he finally became sober, subdued, and hungry. McDonald then took him to a Justice of the Peace where Gordon pled guilty and paid a fine.

Thus was launched the career of one of the most effective law enforcement officers ever known on the Southwest frontier. His later fame reached even the ears of President Theodore Roosevelt, who made it a point to become personally acquainted with Captain Bill.

With respect to George Gordon, this story has an ironic ending. At some time following his run-ins with McDonald, Gordon was attacked and bitten by his own dogs, and he died shortly thereafter, presumably of the wounds received.

Reference:

Albert Bigelow Paine, *Captain Bill McDonald, Texas Ranger* (New York: J. J. Little & Ives Co., 1909).

The Texas Rangers Were Usually, But Not Always, an Exemplary Force

Texans are justifiably proud of their rangers, a unique law enforcement agency that has served the state well. The Texas Rangers trace their history back to 1823 when Stephen F. Austin hired ten men to serve as "rangers." Mounted on horseback, Austin's men were to "range" over certain areas to protect the colonists from Indian depredations. After Texas gained independence from Mexico, the role of the rangers expanded to include protection of citizens and property from Indians and Mexicans, and they participated successfully in numerous skirmishes against both elements. Over the years, the image of the Texas Rangers became the image of a proud, efficient, and fearless law enforcement agency typified by mottos and phrases such as "one riot, one ranger."

The pride with which the rangers have come to be regarded has not always been justified, however. In their formative years, the rangers were charged with patrolling and protecting the borders of the new nation/state. Operating on both sides of the Rio Grande, they were effectively a law unto themselves, and there were times when they were considered to be out of control and more lawless than law abiding. During the Mexican-American War, the rangers were used in various capacities, and they earned the name among the Mexicans as "los Tejanos sangrientos" (the bloody Texans). One incident, at the hacienda of San Francisco de los Patos in Coahuila, serves as an example.

Acting as an escort for twenty supply wagons, a unit of Texas Rangers passed through Patos late one afternoon. After quenching their thirst at the local cantina, the group rode out of town and established camp about a half mile away. One of the rangers, however, remained in the cantina and became thoroughly intoxicated.

Upon finally leaving the cantina, this lone ranger (no pun intended) staggered into the nearby church and ripped down a large wooden crucifix. Dragging the sacred symbol outside, he affixed his rope to it, mounted his horse, and proceeded to gallop around the plaza dragging the crucifix behind him. The astonished Mexican inhabitants of Patos stood transfixed and motionless.

After the ranger ran down an elderly priest who tried to retrieve the crucifix, the astonishment of the citizens turned to horror and rage. Dragging the ranger from his horse, they tied him to a wooden cross in the plaza and began to flog him severely. The ranger's riderless horse left the scene of action and made his way to the encampment; whereupon the other rangers knew that something was wrong.

Galloping into Patos and seeing their comrade's plight, the body of rangers let out yells of fury as they rode into the crowd. Indiscriminately they shot and killed everyone they could as the citizens scurried for protection. Finding their comrade on the verge of death and in great pain, they also shot him to end his suffering.

Following the conflict, the Mexicans emerged and buried their dead. They made complaint to the commander of the army of occupation, but after a brief investigation, it was decided to keep the incident secret, and no punitive actions were taken.

Reference:

Julian Samora, Joe Bernal, & Albert Peña, *Gunpowder Justice: A Reassessment of the Texas Rangers* (Notre Dame: University of Notre Dame Press, 1979).

Texas Ranger Edgar Neal Had No Notches on His Gun

Before the Civil War, the San Saba area in the heart of Texas was peaceful, tranquil, and beautiful. But carpetbagger government after the war changed that environment by permitting and even encouraging lawlessness in the area. Forced to take the law into their own hands, residents of San Saba organized themselves into the "Mob of San Saba." The Mob hung rustlers, evicted claim jumpers, and generally restored law and order in San Saba. But power eventually corrupts, and the Mob eventually became the problem rather than the solution. In self-defense, some of the law-abiding citizens organized an "anti-mob" and appealed to Governor Charles A. Culberson for help. Culberson dispatched four Texas Rangers to San Saba, one of whom was Captain Edgar Thomas Neal.

While highly respected and known for his bravery and integrity, Neal had never killed a man. Although ready on many occasions to fire his weapons, he never had to take such action. Somehow Neal managed to make his arrests peacefully. Two examples show Neal's successful technique.

Assigned to arrest a man named Bill Edmonson, Neal went to the Cottonwood Pond community to find him. Everyone knew that the clannish residents at the Pond would give armed resistance to any attempt to arrest one of their number. Nevertheless, Neal went alone and unarmed. Finding Edmonson plowing corn, Neal went up to him and began a natural conversation.

"Bill, there's been a little trouble concerning the whereabouts of some missing steers. I have a warrant here for you, so I can take you into town where you can explain your side of the matter. Suppose we unhitch your horse and take him and mine to your barn and feed 'em a little corn. Maybe you'd have your woman cook us up a snack as it's a long ride to San Saba."

Mrs. Edmonson fixed the requested meal, and after the two men had eaten, they mounted their horses and started for San Saba with Neal continuing his friendly, informal patter. Edmonson was headed for jail before he realized what was happening.

On another occasion, Neal was sent to the community of Cherokee to arrest D. F. McQuinn, a newspaper editor and a Civil War veteran, who had publicly threatened to kill Francis M. Burns. McQuinn was easily provoked to anger and was considered dangerous. Although advised by friends to take deputies, Neal again went alone and unarmed.

"Mr. McQuinn," Neal said upon meeting his intended prey, "you've been kind enough to publish some nice things about me in your paper for which I'm deeply grateful. I sure would appreciate it if you'd come with me to San Saba and help straighten out a little difficulty which appears to have arisen between you and an old acquaintance."

When McQuinn scoffed at the idea, Neal looked him straight in the eye and said softly but firmly, "I can't think of any reason why you and I should ever permit any trouble to come between us. Can you, sir?"

McQuinn succumbed to Neal's quiet determination, as others had also done, and he went along quietly to jail.

Although ready to use his gun, Neal always tried to avoid the necessity. And he was successful in so doing.

Reference:

William Hancock with Mrs. Edgar Thomas Neal, "...Not a Single Notch!" *True West*, November-December 1959.

Bank Robbery in Wichita Falls Could Be Dangerous

With Captain Bill McDonald and his contingent of Texas Rangers temporarily away from the North Texas area, Elmer "Kid" Lewis and Foster Crawford thought it would be a good time to rob the City National Bank in Wichita Falls. Entering through the back door on the afternoon of February 25, 1896, they approached cashier Frank Dorsey and demanded money. When Dorsey refused to comply, they shot him dead, and in the ensuing melee, they wounded H. H. Langford, the bookkeeper,

Bill McDonald controlling the mob at Wichita Falls

Photo: Public domain

and they almost killed the bank's vice president. The two robbers escaped through the back door with about $410 in cash. Mounting their horses, they galloped to a hiding place in a large thicket east of town. Some of the townspeople quickly formed an ad hoc posse and rode after the robbers in full pursuit but failed to catch up with them.

Captain McDonald, on his way back to Wichita Falls from El Paso, received news of the robbery and murder as he was passing through Bellevue, about twenty miles south of Wichita Falls. He immediately wired the authorities at Wichita Falls to have strong and fast horses ready for him and the four rangers with him.

Changing to fresh mounts in the city, McDonald and his men rode off in the direction the robbers had taken. Crossing a small creek, McDonald's horse stumbled, throwing him into a bed of soft mud. Covered head to foot with the mud, he nevertheless continued the pursuit. The weather was cold, and the trail of the robbers led several times across the Wichita River. McDonald got some of his mud washed off, but the cold weather and the icy water made the pursuers very uncomfortable.

Meeting the returning posse, McDonald got some helpful information. The horses Lewis and Crawford had been riding had given out, and at the point of their guns, they confiscated a pair of Clydesdales from a farmer. Approaching the thicket where they planned to hide out, they had to abandon the Clydesdales and proceed on foot.

With the posse now following, McDonald and his men proceeded on and found the Clydesdales. They knew they were getting close. Dismounting, they also proceeded on foot. McDonald who was still recovering from gunshot wounds received two months earlier, was further weakened by having to wade two more icy streams. But he knew his quarry was close at hand, and he had a job to do.

Sending some men to block the way in case the robbers should try to escape into Indian Territory, McDonald continued on. Finally, coming to another stream, there they were, sitting on the other side with their weapons ready.

As Lewis and Crawford began to raise their weapons, McDonald yelled, "Hold up there!" His own Winchester was pointed right at the two men. McDonald's next order was: "Throw up your hands!" The two robbers were captured without a fight, their hands were bound, and the rangers and posse escorted them back to town.

Because of the intense feelings of reprisal in Wichita Falls, McDonald considered taking his prisoners to Henrietta for safekeeping, but he was persuaded to take them to Wichita Falls. The next day McDonald wanted to take the prisoners to Fort Worth, but the district judge would not allow them to be moved out of Wichita Falls. McDonald protested because he knew what the people of Wichita Falls were likely to do.

"I'll appoint twenty-five men to guard them," the judge said.

As they were now needed elsewhere, McDonald reluctantly accepted the judge's ruling, and he and his men departed. That night a mob formed and were allowed to remove Lewis and Crawford from the jail. They hanged the two men from telephone poles in front of the bank where the robbery and murder had taken place. Lewis and Crawford were buried in the potter's field area of the local cemetery.

Although the episode ended at this point, the story has a postscript. A few years ago (1998) I read a newspaper article about the episode. Unfortunately, I cannot now find the article, and I don't remember the newspaper or the date. But I do remember the contents. After recounting the events, the article went on to say that each year during the Christmas season, fresh flowers are discovered on the graves of Lewis and Crawford. Over the years no one was ever seen depositing the flowers, and their source was unknown. But someone, somewhere, remembered the two men with tender feelings.

Reference:

Albert Bigelow Paine, *Captain Bill McDonald, Texas Ranger* (New York: J. J. Little & Ives Co., 1909).

Some Texas Rangers Suffer an Embarrassment

There is probably nothing that can be more embarrassing than for a Texas Ranger to allow his saddle to be stolen off his horse. But that is exactly what happened to two rangers plus the sheriff who was with them.

Social activities on the frontier were rather rare, and dances, when held, were well publicized and well attended. From miles around, people came dressed in their best clothes for festivities that frequently lasted all night. There were unwritten, but strict, rules of conduct, and for the most part people of all ages and backgrounds mixed harmoniously.

On one such occasion in Kimble County, Texas Ranger Captain Dan W. Roberts and a group of his men were encamped nearby. Roberts granted permission to four of his men to attend a dance in Junction City, about eight miles south of their encampment. Sheriff Joe Clemons, who was in the ranger camp, also attended.

Arriving at the location of the dance, the men tied their horses together but left the saddles on the horses with no one guarding. Returning to their horses about daylight, the sheriff and two of the rangers found their saddles had been stolen. Breaking the news to Captain Dan was not an easy task.

Captain D. W. Roberts' camp

Photo courtesy of Western History Collections, University of Oklahoma Libraries

After asking a few questions, the captain felt he knew who had perpetrated the theft, and he also knew where he expected to find them. Sheriff Clemons, who knew every cow trail in the area, was helpful in guiding the rangers on a twenty-mile trek around Junction City, across the Llano River, and to the suspected location of the thieves.

The next morning about daybreak, the rangers came upon the encampment they were seeking and found the men all asleep. Roberts quietly woke up a young man named Hensley and invited him to have breakfast with the rangers. The "invitation" was so pressing that Hensley did not resist. Despite extensive questioning, Hensley claimed to know nothing about the saddles. About that time one of the rangers brought in another suspect named Beardsley. But Hensley was the man Captain Roberts wanted, and he devised a plan.

After breakfast Roberts told three of his men to stay with Beardsley while he took Hensley up into a nearby cedar break. "After I am out of sight, fire off your guns, turn Beardsley loose, and come join me," he instructed.

Everything went according to plan, and when Hensley heard the guns fire, he turned to Roberts with fear in his eyes saying, "Captain, they have killed that man."

"Now if you know anything about those saddles, you had better tell it quick," Roberts responded.

Pleading for mercy, Hensley took Captain Dan and the rangers to where the saddles had been hidden. Extracting a promise from the nineteen-year-old Hensley to go east to his home and not come back to Texas, Roberts released Hensley and never saw him again. Beardsley was recaptured and sentenced to two years in the penitentiary for a different crime, that of cattle stealing.

Captain Roberts refrained from teasing the rangers for having lost their saddles. It was a sensitive subject and one that mercifully was not reported to headquarters.

Reference:

B. Roberts Lackey, *Stories of the Texas Rangers* (San Antonio: The Naylor Company, 1955).

Sam Bass Had a Generous Nature

Among the general populace Sam Bass was probably the most popular outlaw that Texas ever had. Indeed, he was like a Robin Hood to many of the people with whom he came in contact. Although the Texas Rangers and other law enforcement officials considered Bass to be a scourge and a menace, many early Texans accorded him hero status. Countless stories are told of Bass's humanitarian deeds as well as of his daring bank and train robberies. The three stories included here will help show the humane side of this famous bandit.

On one occasion when Bass and his gang were short of grain for their horses, they stole some shelled corn from a farmer's corncrib. As the men rode back to their camp, corn dribbled from a hole in the sack, enabling the farmer to follow their trail. When he found himself approaching a camp known to be occupied by the Bass gang, the farmer prudently turned around and went back home. Nevertheless, Bass encountered the farmer a few days later and handed him a twenty dollar gold piece, explaining, "I had to have some corn in a hurry the other night."

Another time when Bass and his men were in Stephens County, a posse was being formed to hunt for the gang, and a man named Hunt rode to the Caddo store to recruit some men for the posse. As Hunt approached the store, Sam Bass came walking out carrying a bag of provisions and asked Hunt where he was going.

"I'm going to hunt down Sam Bass," Hunt replied.

"Then you don't need to go any farther. You've found him. What are you going to do with him?"

Responding as prudently as possible, Hunt said, "Nothing, I guess."

"How many children you got?" Bass asked.

Sam Bass at age 16

*Photo courtesy of
Western History Collections,
University of Oklahoma Libraries*

We don't know how many children Hunt claimed, but Bass turned back into the store and brought out a dozen apples, a lot of candy, and some coffee.

"Take these apples and candy to your children, and make yourself a big pot of coffee. And never tell a soul you have seen Sam Bass."

It is reported that Hunt waited thirty years to tell the story.

In the spring of 1878, just before he was killed in Round Rock, Sam Bass bought a new suit of clothes at a dry-goods store in Kaufman. Accepting Sam's payment, the store clerk, Chuck Porter, opened the safe to deposit the money. Sam's eyes naturally gravitated to the open safe and the large sum of money inside.

"Son," he commented, "that is a good deal of money."

Kaufman did not have a bank at that time, and because Mr. Cates, the storeowner, was sick, Porter explained that the money was collecting in the safe until it could be taken to a bank at Terrell.

Bass merely advised Porter not to let anyone else see how much money was in the safe, and then he rode away.

When Bass was killed in Round Rock a few months later in July, he was wearing a suit of clothes purchased from the Cates dry-goods store in Kaufman.

Reference:

J. Frank Dobie, "The Robinhooding of Sam Bass," *True West*,
    July-August 1958.

Mobs Didn't Lynch Anyone While Cooper Wright Was Sheriff

Cooper Wright, short and weighing only 135 pounds, was sheriff at Henrietta in Clay County. What he lacked in size, he made up in brave determination. Wright's greatest test came when a mob managed to get Joe Jessup out of jail and attempted to lynch him.

Joe Jessup's daughter, Kate, had given birth to her second illegitimate child, and Joe had publicly claimed after the first one was born that if it ever happened again, he would kill the new child. Well, Kate eventually had another, and Ma Hutchins, the "good angel" in Henrietta, went out to the Jessup place to take care of Kate and help her get back on her feet. It fell to Ma's husband, Mitch, to report to Sheriff Wright that the new baby was nowhere to be seen.

The next day Wright and his four deputies went out to investigate. The weather was freezing cold. Joe Jessup and his horse were gone, but Kate was there in bed with an old horse blanket for cover, and Ma Hutchins was with her. When told the purpose of the sheriff's visit, Kate began crying, and she could only say, "I just don't know, Mr. Wright. I just don't know."

After what seemed to be a fruitless search, the men were about to leave when Wright noticed some newspapers pasted under the stairs to the loft that were not as faded as the other papers being used to seal cracks in the walls. Cutting through the papers, Wright found the badly battered body of the baby.

Taking the body, Wright and his men made a small coffin and buried the child in the graveyard that night. The ground was so frozen they had to build a fire to thaw it out enough for them to dig the grave.

Joe Jessup was eventually located and put in jail, and the following night a large number of men gathered in town with one thing in mind. Four men were designated to keep Sheriff

Wright out of the way while the others lynched Jessup. Over-powering Wright in his office, the four men took his gun and the keys to the jail, passing the keys to others waiting outside. The small and wiry sheriff waited for his chance, and when it came, he picked up a chair and shattered it on the head of one of his captors. Then using a chair leg as a club, he fought his way past the other three men and dashed to the scene of action outside, picking up a .44 Winchester as he went.

The mob already had a rope around Jessup's neck, and twenty men were in the process of pulling him up when Wright got there.

"Turn loose, you _____! You're not going to hang a man while I'm sheriff."

With Wright's Winchester pointing right at them, the men turned loose of the rope, and Jessup tumbled to the ground. The mob had used a hangman's noose, which meant Jessup was still being choked by a knot that couldn't easily be loosened.

"Somebody give me a knife. Quick!" Wright yelled out.

They got the rope cut just in time, and after a few days under Doc Crew's care, Jessup was safely back in jail. Sheriff Cooper Wright had stood up to the mob and had prevailed.

Following a trial in Clay County, Joe Jessup was sentenced to ten years in prison. At the next election in Clay County, Cooper Wright was unopposed for sheriff. Everyone wanted him back.

Reference:

Herbert M. Timmons, "When Cooper Wright Met the Mob," *True West*, December 1956.

Sheriff Enloe Tricked Outlaws into Surrendering

If you can catch them without shooting at them, your own chances of survival are greatly improved. In the East Texas town of Woodville, Sheriff George Enloe was a master at using ruses and disguises to apprehend lawbreakers during his tenure as sheriff of Tyler County from 1888 to 1898.

Sam Feagin, who had just killed a man, sent word to Sheriff Enloe that if the sheriff was thinking of trying to arrest him, the sheriff should bring his "burying clothes." Learning that Feagin was headed toward the ferry on the Nueces River, Enloe got there first and hid in a nearby skiff. Jumping out just as Feagin was passing by, Enloe got the drop on Feagin and brought him back to Woodville. After serving a short time in jail, Feagin and a fellow prisoner named Ezell succeeded in escaping. Knowing that Feagin's father lived nearby at Hillister, Enloe went to Hillister, hid under the Feagin's house, and learned where to find the younger Feagin by listening to the conversations in the house above. Enloe learned that Feagin and his ally were hiding in an empty house by a nearby mill. Approaching the house, Enloe suddenly found himself facing two guns that were pointing at him. Instantly he began to yell, "Close in on 'em boys! Close in there." In the confusion that occurred as the two criminals tried to see who might be coming at them from the rear, Enloe managed to cover them, handcuff them, and return them to jail.

On another occasion, a Mr. Weatherford who had killed two men at a sawmill below Warren, headed for the Louisiana border, but Enloe got to the Sabine ferry first. The next morning Enloe borrowed an old slouch hat and a horse from a Widow West who lived nearby. Riding toward the river, he started rounding up a few stray cattle with seemingly indifference to everything else. Soon another man, who Enloe recognized to be

121

Weatherford, approached from behind him moving toward the ferry. Appearing as just another cattleman, Enloe let the man catch up with him. Then as they were riding side by side, Enloe shoved his gun into Weatherford's face and arrested him.

Mob violence and lynchings were common in those days, and Enloe had to use all his wits to prevent the lynching of one of his prisoners. Green Gilder, a former slave, had killed a white woman at Warren, and a mob was forming with intentions of hanging the killer. To protect the prisoner, Enloe sent him under guard into the woods near the house of Enloe's brother-in-law. Not knowing that the prisoner had been moved, the mob arrived at Enloe's home and demanded the keys to the jail. Nannie Enloe, George's small and dainty wife, defied the mob and threw the keys into a churn of buttermilk. Despite threats from the mob to take Enloe's life, George and Nannie stalled long enough for the guards to get Gilder safely hidden in the woods. George then reached into the buttermilk and gave the keys to the mob.

In several other incidents, Sheriff George Enloe either fooled the lawbreakers or persuaded them, through reasoning, to surrender. He took his job seriously, and he was successful in upholding the law. He also lived to an old age.

Reference:

Lou Ella Mosley, *Pioneer Days of Tyler County* (Ft. Worth: Miran Publishers, 1975).

Jeff Milton was Hired to Clean Up El Paso

Some frontier gunslingers were mean; some were simply tough. Jeff Milton was tough. Some gunslingers were outlaws; some were law enforcers. Milton was a law enforcer—most of the time. Although he roamed throughout the Southwest, Milton spent the majority of his adult years in Texas making other gunslingers back down.

Jeff Milton was born in Florida in 1861. Milton's father, governor of Florida at the time of the boy's birth, was such a passionate supporter of secession that he named the new arrival Jefferson Davis Milton after the president of the Confederacy. Jeff's father committed suicide during Jeff's early teenage years, and Jeff acquired some of his toughness by helping his mother secure the family property from would-be encroachers.

Growing restless and longing for greater adventure, Milton migrated to Texas at the age of sixteen, and he joined the Texas Rangers, claiming to be twenty-one. A Texas Ranger had to have a reputation of being ready to fight at any time, and Milton was no exception. In one encounter with an outlaw named Dorsey who was resisting arrest, Milton asserted, "Let me tell you something, Dorsey. You either come with me, or you get killed and I'll pull you in." Realizing that Milton was not bluffing, Dorsey came peacefully.

After three years as a ranger, Milton became restless again and

Jeff D. Milton
Photo courtesy of Western History Collections, University of Oklahoma Libraries

moved on to Fort Davis and then to Murphyville, which later became Alpine, Texas. On one occasion as a deputy sheriff in Murphyville, Milton walked into a saloon and confronted a group of cowboys who had been boasting that they would run the law out of town. With a twelve-gauge shotgun in his hands, Milton said "Boys, every one of you get your six-shooters off as fast as you can or I'll kill every one of you right here." Again, Milton prevailed.

Continuing to drift, Milton served as deputy sheriff in Socorro County, New Mexico, where he fought his way out of ambush by killing three Mexican bandits. Having been shot in the leg by one of the bandits, Milton poured turpentine into the wound and then rode back to town. Milton had additional exploits as he served for a time as a member of the U.S. Border Patrol.

El Paso, in those days, was the bawdy gathering place for the lawless and immoral elements of frontier society. In an effort to start cleaning up the city in 1894, the city fathers looked for the toughest man they could find to become chief of police. They hired Jeff Milton.

The constable in El Paso at the time was a man named John Selman, the same John Selman who later gained fame by shooting and killing John Wesley Hardin. Although a law enforcement officer, Selman and his deputy were accepting protection money from many of the undesirable business establishments. They were not happy about Milton's presence, and Selman began boasting about "where he would stick this young upstart's gun." Taking the initiative, Milton confronted Selman, challenging him to make good his boast, but Selman declined the opportunity. Milton then advised the deputy to stop taking bribes.

Because the two men continued receiving protection money, Milton had to confront them again. "If you try it again, I'll put you both in jail. And if either of you starts anything with me again, I'm going to kill you, certain." Milton had no further trouble with Selman or from his deputy.

On another occasion Milton had an encounter with a rather large man who worked as a bouncer in some of the more unsavory saloons in town. When the bouncer threatened Milton, Jeff grabbed him by the ear, kicked him, and sent him sprawling into the street. Picking himself up, the bouncer found himself looking into the muzzle of Milton's Colt revolver. "Next time you speak to me, come up and take your hat off. And don't pass me on the street without taking your hat off—at no time!"

Things became relatively peaceful in El Paso for a while. Some accounts have Milton engaging in an eye-to-eye confrontation with John Wesley Hardin who came to El Paso with the initial intent of practicing law instead of gunmanship. Seeing Hardin in a saloon wearing his pistol belt, Milton approached and told Hardin to check his guns at the bar.

"Do you know who you are talking to?" Hardin asked.

"I evidently do, sir, and I think if I were you, I'd take them off right now, before anything starts," Milton responded.

The two eyed each other for a moment, and then Hardin acquiesced. "All right, chief. We'll abide by the law."

Things continued to go well for Milton until one night in June 1895 when he was involved in shooting a fugitive, Martin Morose, who was returning to El Paso from Juarez. Milton and Deputy U.S. Marshal George Scarborough ordered Morose to surrender. It was claimed that Morose went for his guns and immediately fell under the fire from Milton and Scarborough. Several of the townspeople, however, took exception to the report, and they felt that the shooting should be considered a murder rather than an act of self-defense. The accusations persisted until finally, both Milton and Scarborough decided to leave El Paso.

Drifting over to Arizona, Milton's last known escapade was in Tombstone, in a Model T Ford, when he chased a bank robber who was fleeing on foot. For a couple of miles it was an even chase, but then the robber, Fred Koch, began tiring before the Model T did. Again, Jeff Milton got his man.

Near the end of his life, Milton expressed his philosophy in simple terms. "I never killed a man who didn't need killing; I never shot an animal except for meat."

Reference:

Robert Barr Smith, "Jefferson Davis Milton," *Wild West*, August 1994.

Ben Thompson Took Time to Aim in Self-Defense

Several western gunslingers claimed that they never killed anyone except in self-defense. But many times they brought on the incidents that led to the need for self-defense. Take Ben Thompson for example.

British-born Ben Thompson was considered to be just as good with a gun as Wild Bill Hickok, but fortunately the two never had to confront one another. With a short-fused temper, Thompson was continually getting into scrapes, and people lost count of the number of men he had killed. Although he spent a lot of time getting his brother, Billy, out of trouble, Thompson made his own trouble on many occasions.

In Austin, Texas, Thompson liked to frequent The Senate, a saloon owned by Mark Wilson. On one occasion, while drinking heavily, Thompson found himself losing money at the saloon's monte table. Voices grew loud as Thompson accused the dealer of cheating. Wilson, an Irishman who also had a quick temper, came over to calm the situation.

"I don't like the way this man deals," Thompson growled.

Ben Thompson as Austin city marshal

Photo courtesy of G. U. Hubbard Collection

"Then why don't you leave," Wilson suggested.

"I'll leave when I get _____ good and ready! This is a public saloon even if you do own it."

"I'm asking you to leave, Thompson, and stay away."

The saloon became very quiet as the other patrons waited with bated breath to see what would happen next. Their expectations did not materialize at that time, as Thompson decided to leave. But at the saloon's door, Thompson turned, whipped out his pistol, and shot at a large overhead chandelier, sending it crashing to the floor.

The next day when he was more sober, Thompson decided he would go back to The Senate to apologize and pay for the chandelier. Letting his intentions be known, he instructed a friend: "You tell Wilson that at four sharp, I'm entering the front door of The Senate."

Entering the saloon as advertised, Thompson yelled to the bartender, "Where's your boss. I came back to show him I wasn't afraid of him last night."

At that moment, Wilson appeared on the upper landing to the "girls' quarters." "I told you never to come back," Wilson yelled as he fired at Thompson with a shotgun. The pellets hit the wall behind Thompson, who instantly had his gun out and in action. Receiving four of Thompson's bullets, Wilson toppled dead to the floor below. Making the mistake of grabbing a Winchester behind the bar and firing at Thompson, the bartender became Thompson's next target and was fatally wounded.

Onlookers said that the whole affair lasted no more than five seconds. Handing his smoking gun to one of the terrified patrons, Thompson said, "Somebody go for the marshal. I came in here a peaceful citizen to pay for the damage I caused last night. I shot in defense of my life. They both shot first."

A coroner's jury convened an hour later and acquitted Thompson, ruling that he had indeed acted in self-defense. Later when asked how he had managed to prevail over two men who had shot first, Thompson explained that shooting first does not win a gunfight unless you also take time to aim. "Those men shot too fast," he said.

Ben Thompson eventually changed roles and became city marshal of Austin, Texas. Law-breakers and other gunslingers stayed out of his way.

Reference:

Lew Smith, "Take Your Time—And Aim!" *True West*, September-October 1958.

Kind Words Come from a Bad Man

When it comes to deciding who was the "baddest" of the bad men of the American West, John Wesley Hardin's name has to be among the leaders. He may not have achieved the fame of the likes of Jesse James or Wild Bill Hickok or Billy the Kid, but none of these people came close to Hardin's record of killings. History says that Hardin killed about forty people during his lifetime. He was loved by a few, hated by many, and feared by all. He had a very short fuse. It is claimed that he shot a man whose snoring was keeping him awake one night.

After serving sixteen years in prison for murdering a deputy sheriff, Hardin was released in 1889. He attempted to practice law, but liquor and all-night card games thwarted his attempts to reform. He migrated to El Paso, the wildest gambling town in Texas at that time.

Early in the afternoon of August 19, 1895, an eleven-year-old telegraph delivery boy found Hardin in the Acme Saloon on San Antonio Street. This young lad had delivered

several telegrams to Hardin that summer, and he generally knew where to find him. And Hardin always treated the boy kindly. As the lad walked into the saloon, Hardin was at the bar raising a large glass of whiskey to his lips.

"Another telegram for you, Mr. Hardin."

John Wesley Hardin

Photo courtesy of Western History Collections, University of Oklahoma Libraries

Hardin lowered the glass to the bar, put his hand on the lad's head, and said, "Son, don't ever do this." He then reached into his trousers pocket, took out a dime, and gave it to the boy.

"I won't sir," the boy promised. "Thank you." He turned and went on his way.

Toward midnight that evening, Hardin was in a drunken brawl in the Wigwam Saloon farther up the street, when he was shot in the back of the head and killed. The telegraph delivery boy went to the undertaker's parlor as soon as he could get off work the next day to see Hardin's body and to pay last respects to the man who had been kind to him.

We may never know the contents of the telegram, but we do know that the delivery boy heeded Hardin's advice. That delivery boy grew up, married, and became my father. Whenever he would tell the story, he would usually end by saying, "Thus ended the life of a desperado who had been universally feared. Yet I received only kindnesses from him."

Reference:

Personal recollection of Dr. Louis H. Hubbard, the telegraph boy.

It Took Two Hangings to End Bill Longley's Life

Not many people can claim to have been hanged twice. Being hanged once is bad enough, and the result is usually very final. But William Preston Longley, known more simply as Bill, survived a hanging and lived to be hanged again.

Growing up in Evergreen, Texas, Bill became an excellent marksman. It was said by some that he could hit any target from a galloping horse. During his teenage and early adult years, Longley was involved in several shooting scrapes around Evergreen and throughout Texas. Over a ten-year period, he was credited with over thirty killings—mostly federal soldiers, Northern sympathizers, and posse members. A posse finally caught up with Longley, and upon capturing him, they hanged him from the limb of a tree.

As Longley dangled from the noose, the posse members took shots at him. The first shot bounced off a gold belt around Longley's waist, and the second shot cut most of the strands of the rope around Longley's neck. As the posse rode away, a thirteen-year-old boy cut the rest of the rope, and Longley tumbled to the ground, still alive.

Recovering, Longley soon exacted retribution on one of

William P. Longley

Photo courtesy of Western History Collections, University of Oklahoma Libraries

the posse members by hanging him from the same tree. This time it was Longley who fired shots into a dangling body, and his shots were right on the mark.

After being away for some time, Longley returned to Evergreen with the intent of killing Wilson Anderson, who Longley believed had murdered Longley's cousin. Captured and jailed, Longley was tried in Giddings, the county seat, and he was sentenced again to be hanged. While awaiting his execution, Longley wrote a letter in which he complained of his unfair treatment since John Wesley Hardin, an equally prolific and notorious killer, had gotten off with only a twenty-five-year sentence. The plea fell on deaf ears, however, and the second hanging took place.

An old-timer in Giddings, who later recalled witnessing the hanging, reported Longley's last words of contriteness: "I see a lot of enemies out there and mighty few friends. I deserve this fate. It is a debt I owe for my wild reckless life. Goodbye, everybody."

Bill Longley was hanged until dead. He was only twenty-seven years old.

Reference:

Ann Ruff, *Amazing Texas Monuments & Museums* (Houston: Lone Star Books, 1984).

Someone Shot the Portrait as Well as the Man

The murder of Thomas Jefferson Chambers has never been solved. In fact, there is an eeriness about it that makes one wonder.

A native of Virginia, Chambers came to Texas shortly before the Texas Revolution and settled in the picturesque southeast Texas community of Anahuac (pronounced AN-A-WAK). Sitting on a bluff overlooking the Gulf of Mexico, Anahuac was initially a Spanish settlement and later a port of entry for American colonists. Chambers came via Mexico to claim land grants awarded him for various services rendered to the Mexican government.

Chambers was a man of many talents and was skilled as a surveyor and a lawyer. In 1829 he served as Surveyor General of Texas, and he was appointed sole Superior Judge of Texas before 1836. During Texas's war for independence from Mexico, Chambers obtained the title of "general" while serving the Texas side as a recruiting officer and by being a gun runner. Serving again as a judge after Texas gained independence, he

Thomas Jefferson Chambers' home at Anahuac

Photo courtesy of G. U. Hubbard Collection

also became a busy land speculator. In 1861 he was a member of the Texas Secession Convention.

While living in Anahuac, Chambers built an elegant two-story house, located a block away from the present county courthouse. Overhead eaves projecting from the roof sheltered a front porch and a back porch. A winding staircase on the front porch gave access to the upper floor, and a star-shaped window in a gable on the south side gave a view of the Gulf. A full-length portrait of Chambers hung on a wall in an upper room on the south side of the house.

One day in 1865, as Chambers was standing in the room containing his portrait, someone fired a shot through the second story window. The bullet passed through Chambers' body and lodged in his portrait on the wall. The citizens of Anahuac thought it very singular that the bullet that killed him struck the portrait in exactly the same place it had passed through his body. Thus a special aura of mystery became associated with the murder, which has given a basis for much speculation and conversation over the subsequent years. Although many theories have been advanced as to the identity of the culprit, the crime remains unsolved.

Reference:

F. M. McCarty, *Texas Guidebook* (Amarillo: The F. M. McCarty Company, 1970).

Building the Railroads

Introduction

With its virtually unlimited natural resources, Texas was initially a heaven for agrarian and livestock industries. The seemingly inexhaustible piney woods of East Texas supported a lucrative lumber industry. The innumerable herds of cattle in the west made Texas a leading cattle state. In between, Central Texas provided the right environments for raising cotton and other crops. Although the resources were plentiful and virtually available for the asking, the tasks of getting them to market presented major challenges.

Cattle drives to the north and river routes to the Gulf of Mexico were the principle means of getting produce to market. The cattle could walk to the railheads, which were mostly in Kansas. Cotton and lumber and other commodities were taken to river ports and then by ship to the eastern markets. When the railroads came, they ushered in a new era of commercial transportation.

As the railroads built into Texas from the north and the east, they not only brought in additional settlers, they gave rise to two major marketing changes. Cattle drives to the railheads in Kansas were no longer necessary; the trains now came to the cattle. The other change was that rail transport virtually replaced river transport. Shipping centers on rivers declined or died, and new shipping centers were created along railroad right-of-ways.

The railroads, a major industry in and of themselves, changed the whole scheme of getting goods to market. They also accelerated the migration of settlers into Texas and throughout all the western frontier.

The Pecos High Bridge Was an Early Engineering Marvel

The initial route of the Southern Pacific Railroad going east from El Paso followed a tortuously crooked route as it approached the Pecos River. Because of the curves and mountainous terrain, trains in that area had to move very slowly. Studying the situation, Jim Converse, chief construction engineer of the Southern Pacific in that area, conceived an alternate route that would eliminate two tunnels and shorten the railroad by eleven miles.

Construction of the new route began in 1891. Many laborers were required, and three frog towns came into existence. (Frog towns were those tent cities that hopped along with the tracks as the railroads pushed through the frontier.) Converse's new route would require a bridge 2,180 feet long and towering 321 feet above the Pecos River, a bridge higher and more massive than any other that had thus far been undertaken in America, and the construction would be quite dangerous.

The work went slowly but smoothly until an accident occurred in which seven men were killed. Three others were severely injured and not expected to recover. Judge Roy

Judge Roy Bean
Photo courtesy of Western History Collections, University of Oklahoma Libraries

Bean was summoned from Langtry to perform the inquest, as was the custom in that area at the time. Bean made the death pronouncements, then, being in a hurry to get back to Langtry, he looked briefly at the three injured men and, pronouncing them dead also, made his departure.

Upon completion of the Pecos High Bridge, as it came to be known, the trains ran on a much-improved schedule as Converse had predicted. But when the new route was only two weeks old, C. P. Huntington, owner of the Southern Pacific, surprised everyone by ordering it closed and rerouting the trains back to their original slow route. Reasons for this unexpected turn of events are unclear. One theory is that Huntington wanted to discourage the other people who had invested in the bridge and then reopen it after they had dropped out, thus garnering all the profits to himself. Another theory is that he wanted to bargain with the federal government for greater concessions and was holding back the new route as leverage.

Regardless of Huntington's reasons, the new route eventually reopened and remained in use for many years. Passage over the bridge was safe yet frightening, especially when the bridge swayed with the wind. On more than one occasion, train passengers walked across in fear that their train might be blown off by the winds.

In 1910 the bridge was reinforced, and then in 1944, having served its purpose successfully, it was replaced by a newer bridge made of concrete and steel.

Reference:

Jack Skiles, *Judge Roy Bean Country* (Lubbock: Texas Tech University Press, 1996).

The Katy Railroad Intended for These Engines to Collide

The Missouri-Kansas-Texas (Katy) Railroad faced stiff competition as it built southward into Texas. The Santa Fe, Frisco, and Rock Island Railroads were also pursuing the lucrative business of transporting passengers, livestock, and freight between Texas and the eastern markets.

In hopes of increasing passenger traffic and revenues, W. G. Crush, general passenger agent for the Katy, conceived a scheme calculated to attract attention to his line. He would stage a train wreck. And to have a proper place to do it, he would create a town along the line, and excursion trains would bring the people. Thus the town of Crush City, Texas, was born.

Restaurants, first aid stations, saloons, and a jail were established. Duly authorized officers of the law were sworn in. Huge billboards along the Katy's right-of-way and advertisements in scores of newspapers told of the coming event. The advertising was effective, for on the appointed day, Crush City had a population of 30,000 people. The saloons and the jail did a thriving business, and the police officers stayed busy.

The exhibition was to take place in a basin about a quarter of a mile wide. Gently rolling hills on either side made an excellent amphitheater for spectators. The two participating engines were face to face on the main line, each pulling a tender and six box cars. The plan called first for a dry run, and then for the real thing.

The engineers backed their trains up until they were two miles apart, and at the signal, they raced down the track toward each other with whistles blowing. Then the brakes shrieked as steel slid on steel, and the crowd gasped in genuine apprehension as the two trains barely managed to stop with their cow catchers clanking together. For a dry run, it was much too close for comfort.

Now it was time for the real thing. After a lengthy pause for picture taking, the engineers backed their trains up and again awaited the signal. This time they were going to collide at full speed. Throwing their throttles wide open, the two engineers jumped to safety as the trains gathered speed, and the two trains came together with a mighty crash. One of the boilers exploded, clouds of dust enveloped the scene, and broken metal flew everywhere. Two spectators were struck and killed by flying metal, and several others were injured. It was a rather subdued crowd that climbed aboard the excursion trains to return home.

W. G. Crush had to admit that the scheme was not as successful as he had hoped. Although 30,000 passengers in the excursion trains brought good revenue to the Katy, many of them also brought lawsuits. Crush succeeded in getting publicity for the railroad, but most of the publicity was less than favorable.

Despite the tragic results of the Crush City spectacle, train wrecks were also staged on other railroads as publicity stunts. As far as can be determined, the Katy's episode was the only time a railroad staged a wreck in the United States and succeeded in continuing in business afterward. The Katy weathered the aftermath of the episode and became a very successful railroad in Texas.

Reference:

Paul Norton, "Train Wrecks Made to Order," *Railway Progress*, May 1953.

It Took a While, but the Train Finally Got There

Railroad trains in America have earned a reputation of frequently arriving late. While not always deserved, this reputation has inspired a plethora of jokes and tales of woe about railroad performance. Normally one thinks of train delays in terms of hours, but there is one case on record of a delay measured in years.

Around the turn of the century, the Gulf & Interstate Railroad ran between Beaumont, Texas and Port Bolivar, where it served the Galveston Bay area. On the morning of September 7, 1900, Train No. 1, a mixed train of passengers and freight, left Beaumont with every expectation of reaching Port Bolivar the next morning. The trip was uneventful and the train was proceeding on schedule until crossing High Island about eleven miles east of Port Bolivar. That was when a gigantic storm surge hit Galveston, destroying property, killing thousands, and forever changing the economic preeminence of the city.

As the water struck the overall area, the train was one of the casualties. The engine and tender were half buried in sand. The baggage car was swept 500 feet inland. The crew and

The Gulf & Interstate Railroad Depot at Beaumont

Photo courtesy of Tyrrell Historical Library, Beaumont, Texas

141

passengers were able to extricate themselves, however, with no loss of life.

Thirty miles of track were gone, and the railroad's management did not have the funds needed to put it all back together. Finally, three years later, the citizens of Beaumont and Galveston raised $20,000, and repairs were begun. The line was rebuilt, and the engine was taken back to Beaumont where it was refurbished and repainted. Then it resumed its journey.

The G&I offered to honor the tickets of any passenger who still wanted to make the trip to Port Bolivar, and several such persons showed up to "resume" the trip. This time Train No. 1 made it all the way to Port Bolivar, arriving at 11:10 A.M. on September 24, 1903—a total of three years, sixteen days, and ten minutes late.

It is said that one of the original passengers stormed into a Port Bolivar restaurant asking, "Aren't those three-minute eggs done yet?"

Reference:

W. Somerville, "Comin' Down the Railroad," *The Saturday Evening Post*, September 15, 1928.

How to Run a Railroad Without an Engine

The Memphis, El Paso & Pacific Railroad was one of those short line railroads that did whatever it took to stay in operation. Enterprise and ingenuity were necessary ingredients for survival as America moved westward, and the MEP&P did not intend to be left behind.

At the end of the Civil War, this forty-mile railroad that ran between Marshall, Texas and Shreveport, Louisiana found itself with only three boxcars and no engines. The war had stripped the line of everything else. But the railroad's management was determined to keep operating, and they found a way to run their three-car train tri-weekly between Marshall and Shreveport without the usual motive power.

How did they do it? They loaded a team of oxen into the first boxcar, freight and passengers into the second car, and train crew and management into the third car. Gravity would permit an eastbound train to coast out of Marshall along a long downgrade. At the bottom of the downgrade, the oxen would be brought out and hitched to the front of the train, and they would pull the train to the top of the next hill. Then, with the oxen back in the lead car, the train would again coast as far as it could. In this manner the eastbound trains made the trips to Shreveport, and the westbound trains negotiated the return forty miles. With gravity for the downgrades and oxen for the level areas and the upgrades, the little railroad managed to operate in both directions on a timely and consistent schedule.

The passenger fare was twenty-five cents; freight charges were anything the owner could get. As soon as the three-car train arrived at its destination and unloaded, it was quickly available for reloading and a return trip. With no competition on that particular route, the MEP&P conducted a profitable business.

Reference:

B. A. Botkin, *A Treasury of Railroad Folklore* (New York: Bonanza Books, 1953).

The Fredericksburg and Northern Railroad Tried Its Best

The tracks of the Fredericksburg and Northern Railroad (F&N) ran south from Fredericksburg down to Fredericksburg Junction, twenty-four miles away. This anomaly between the railroad's name and its direction typifies the various inconsistencies of its checkered life.

Fredericksburg wanted a railroad, as did Kerrville and many other towns in the Texas hill country. But railroad construction in the hill country was considered to be an expensive and risky venture by the larger railroads, who chose to build around the hill country rather than through it. Being unable to entice any of the existing railroad companies to build into Fredericksburg, the Germanic citizens of that community raised the necessary funds and built their own railroad.

Raising $400,000, the promoters built the twenty-four-mile line in eleven months in 1913. Connecting to the San Antonio and Aransas Pass Railroad at Fredericksburg Junction, a direct rail route was now established between San Antonio and Fredericksburg. The two-week trip by wagon between the two cities would be reduced to one day. The $125 shipping cost of a wagonload of granite would be reduced to $20. Prospects were bright and exciting.

The reality, however, was a different story, and the railroad's first day of operation foreshadowed that which was to come. To commemorate the arrival of the first train into their city, the citizens of Fredericksburg planned a gala three-day celebration. Townspeople and farming families gathered from miles around to witness the arrival of the first train. The train arrived, but it came in an hour late, and after it came to a halt, one of the farmers went up to the engine as though it were a real horse instead of an iron horse, and patting it tenderly, said, "Poor thing. You must be very tired." The gala celebration didn't go any better, as heavy rains came and caused the cancellation of many of the planned activities.

Throughout its brief life, the F&N was plagued with problems and inconsistencies. Because the roadbed was built over a terrain of soft limestone, it would settle during rainstorms, and in places it even sank out of sight. Derailments were common, with a dozen occurring during one trip. Average speed on the line was only twelve miles an hour, and sometimes eighteen hours were required to make the twenty-four-mile trip. Ticket agents always warned passengers to bring along a supply of food as a precautionary measure. It was sometimes irreverently said that a passenger would have to begin the journey in August in order to reach the end of the line by Christmas.

On one occasion, rains washed away a bridge just minutes after a train had crossed it, and the rushing torrent also washed away the next bridge ahead of the train, thus isolating the train. The crew and passengers trudged to a nearby farmhouse where they obtained overnight accommodations from a generous farmer.

One of the engineering marvels on the line was a 200-foot-long tunnel under the crest of the divide between the Pedernales and the Guadalupe Rivers. The builders were proud of their tunnel, the only railroad tunnel in Texas at that time. But instead of speeding traffic over that section of the line, the tunnel was often a bottleneck. Rocks falling from above frequently blocked the track, and in the winter, icicles a foot thick protruded downward from the tunnel's ceiling, completely blocking the trains until knocked away. (The abandoned tunnel now serves as home for a large colony of Mexican bats.)

Other problems also beset the railroad. Frequently, the engines ran out of water, and the crew would have to pump water from nearby streams or ponds. Pools of water were always available at the tunnel. Crews would also have to go into the woods and cut trees when the engine's fuel supply ran low. When one of the trestles caught fire, all employees, including the general manager, jumped on handcars and raced down the tracks to fight the fire.

The F&N struggled along for twenty-eight years before finally giving way to highways and more modern modes of transportation. As it went into the scrap heap, it became merely a nostalgic memory of the old-timers.

Reference:

Richard Zelade, *Hill Country* (Houston: Gulf Publishing Company, 1997).

Charley Wilson Took on the Southern Pacific and Won

Charley Wilson was smart—smart enough to figure out that the Southern Pacific Railroad, building eastward from El Paso, would want to establish a division headquarters about halfway between El Paso and San Antonio. As a member of a U.S. Army detachment protecting the railroad construction crews, Charley managed to examine maps of the railroad's surveyors, and he was sure that the proposed station of Strawbridge would become the expected headquarters. Applying for a discharge from the army, Charley rushed to Austin and purchased Section 4, Block 151 in Pecos County. In 1882, when the railroad made Strawbridge a division point and began work on a roundhouse, Charley Wilson was in possession of all the land surrounding the railroad's right-of-way.

After having been given free lands all along the route, the Southern Pacific officials were furious upon learning that they would have to purchase land from Wilson for their station, freight office, and sidings in Strawbridge. To make matters worse, Charlie erected a large tent next to the station to serve as a restaurant and saloon. Wilson got so much business from passengers and railroad workers that he replaced the tent with an adobe building that became known as the Cottage Bar. Complaining that the Cottage Bar was having a detrimental effect on the efficiency of its work crews, the railroad officials set about to get rid of the establishment.

Resurveying the area, the railroad determined that a portion of the Cottage Bar was actually on railroad property, and the division superintendent publicly ordered Charley to close it. One can imagine the superintendent's surprise when Charley agreed without complaint.

Now, one can imagine the superintendent's greater surprise a few days later upon learning that Charlie was building a new saloon inside one end of the railroad's roundhouse. "That portion of the roundhouse is on my property," claimed Charlie, who had made his own survey. "I have a right to build on my own property."

The division superintendent had no recourse but to compromise with Charlie Wilson. If he would leave their roundhouse alone, they would leave his Cottage Bar alone. In addition, they gave the Cottage Bar unlimited free water from the railroad's water tank. Wilson had beaten the mighty Southern Pacific.

The name of Strawbridge was changed to Sanderson, and Charlie Wilson, who had also platted the town and sold lots became known as the "father" of Sanderson, Texas. Wilson added to his fortunes by being instrumental in having Sanderson declared county seat of the newly created Terrell County.

Reference:

Roy D. Holt, "Feuding with the Southern Pacific," *Frontier Times*, April-May 1975.

Politicians, Leaders, and Entrepreneurs

Introduction

The challenge of the Rockies to "bring me men to match my mountains" can easily be reworded as a call from Texas to "bring me men to match my resources."

The men came! They came from the eastern and northern but mostly from the southern states of America. They came from England, Ireland, France, Germany, and many other European nations. And for the most part, they overcame the challenges and seized the opportunities.

The American West attracted the hardy, the adventurous, the doers. Those less inclined to the required rugged and precarious life of the frontier stayed home or went back home. Cattle and agriculture attracted the first settlers. Then discovery of oil at Spindletop created an additional industry of international importance, and for a long time Texas was the petroleum capital of the world.

Just as Texas produced and received goods and commerce, Texas also produced leaders and entrepreneurs—men who made things happen. The economic climate was right, and men of daring and foresight took advantage of it. Outstanding leaders emerged in large numbers among the many men who came to Texas for adventure or for opportunity. Politicians, statesmen, soldiers, and entrepreneurs rose to the occasion in their new land of opportunity. For the most part, they attained greatness within the borders of Texas. But in addition, Texas also produced men who went elsewhere to achieve greatness and then returned to devote their talents and energies to their home state.

Sam Houston Takes Issue with the Utah Expedition

In 1857 President James Buchanan ordered the U.S. Army to march to the Territory of Utah to quell a supposed insurrection of the Mormons in the newly organized territory. Now what, if anything, does that episode have to do with Texas? It turned out that Sam Houston, a U.S. Senator from Texas, became one of the most vocal critics of the expedition.

The expedition, which came to be known as "Johnston's Army," was initially commanded by General William S. Harney. Becoming needed elsewhere, Harney left the expedition while en route and was replaced by Colonel Albert Sidney Johnston.

Sympathizing somewhat with the Mormon reactions to the inhumane treatment by corrupt and autocratic federal officials in their territory, Sam Houston decried the sending of the army. In an oration on the Senate floor, Houston suggested that instead of having sent an army, "why not send them men to whom they could unbosom themselves." He further suggested that if the United States would send "honest men and gentlemen, whose morals, whose wisdom, and whose character, comport with the high station they fill," that the Mormons would likely be willing to surrender to them and act in obedience with the laws of the United States.

Houston was especially incensed by one incident that occurred just outside of Utah. Being bogged down for the winter and running out of supplies, the army was in a state of severe hardship. Salt was especially needed by their cattle. Learning of the situation, Brigham Young sent a large supply of salt out to the army with the message that it was a free gift, but if the commander preferred, he could pay a fair price later. Being loath to accept anything from the "rebellious Mormons," the Union commander refused to accept the salt at all.

153

Portrait of Sam Houston in lobby
of Texas State Archives
*Photo courtesy of G. U. Hubbard
Collection*

To Houston, refusing the salt, besides being an act of needless discourtesy, meant that if the soldiers had to resort to eating their cattle, the unsalted meat could produce cholera, which might be especially fatal to men in tents in such severe winter weather.

Continuing his oration on the Senate floor, Houston said, "What was the message the military officer sent back? I believe the substance of it was that he would have no intercourse with a rebel, and that when they met they would fight. They will fight; and if they fight, he (the commander) will get miserably whipped. That was a time to make peace with Brigham Young, because there is something potent in salt. It is the sacrament of perpetual friendship."

Peaceful arrangements finally prevailed, and Johnston's army was allowed into the Salt Lake Valley the following spring without shots being fired. Brigham Young accepted the new territorial governor appointee, Alfred Cumming, as an honest and fair-minded man, and the supposed rebellion existed no more. When the U.S. government policies and actions became consistent with Sam Houston's expressed views, peace and harmony prevailed.

Reference:

Writings of Sam Houston, 1858, in Texas Archives, Austin, Texas.

Were Richard Bullock's Pigs Worth 35 Million French Francs?

In 1840 the Republic of Texas was hoping to borrow 35 million francs from France until some marauding pigs initiated events that put an end to the negotiations.

Count Alphonse de Saligny came to Texas in 1839 as France's representative to the new republic. Although he saw the economic potential of this new country, Saligny did not relate well with the rough and crude ways of the frontiersmen with whom he was now associating. And he was especially bothered by a group of pigs belonging to an Austin innkeeper, Richard Bullock.

Although the grounds and gardens of the French embassy were fenced, the pigs frequently forced their way onto the property to eat the corn reserved for the horses. Saligny reported that on one occasion, a dozen pigs burst into the stable and frightened eight horses that completely wrecked the stable in their frenzy. On another occasion Saligny claimed that three pigs entered his bedroom, ate his linens, and destroyed his papers. Saligny further complained that his servants spent two hours every morning repairing the fence and that 140 pounds of nails had thus far been used. But still, the pigs worked their way in.

French Legation Embassy

Photo courtesy of G. U. Hubbard Collection

Finally in desperation, Saligny ordered one of his servants to kill some of the pigs. Upon finding his slain pigs, Bullock became so angered that he physically attacked the servant and pounded him severely with his fists. To Saligny, such an act toward the Charge d'affaires of the King of France and his servants was an "odious violation of the law of nations," and he demanded that Bullock be punished consistently with "the enormity of the offense."

Count de Saligny
Photo courtesy of Center for American History, University of Texas at Austin

Bullock was arrested and then released on bond, claiming that Saligny should have built a better fence. This hardly satisfied Saligny, and after his further complaints reached the Texas Secretary of State, Bullock was re-arrested but again released. Because of failure to pay some of his past debts and the passing of bogus promissory notes, Saligny did not have public opinion on his side.

All this could have passed as a humorous set of occurrences except for one thing. Saligny's brother-in-law was the French Minister of Finance. The loan of 35 million francs that Texas sought was not granted.

References:

June Rayfield Welch, *Historic Sites of Texas* (Dallas: Yellow Rose Press, 1972).

Nancy Nichols Barker, *The French Legation in Texas, Vol. 1: Recognition, Rupture, and Reconciliation* (Austin: Texas State Historical Association, 1971).

General Albert Sidney Johnston Was a Hero to Texans

Texans love to idolize their heroes, and names like Austin, Houston, Travis, Bowie, Fannin, Rusk, and others are well known to students of Texas history as the heroic leaders of Texans in the formative stages of the republic and state. General Albert Sidney Johnston is another who was accorded heroic status.

An 1826 graduate from the U.S. Military Academy at West Point, Johnston was considered to be a brilliant young officer. In 1834 he resigned his commission and took up farming in order to care for his seriously ill wife, who died shortly thereafter. Following her death, Johnston met Stephen F. Austin, who persuaded him to come to Texas.

Although the war between Texas and Mexico was over when Johnston arrived in Nacogdoches in July 1836, the Texas army was filled with volunteers from the East who were anxious to wreak vengeance on Mexico and Santa Anna. Johnston joined the unruly Texas army as a private, but the commanding general, Thomas Jefferson Rusk, quickly promoted Johnston to

Albert Sidney Johnston grave at Texas State Cemetery

Photo courtesy of G. U. Hubbard Collection

adjutant general. Sam Houston, in New Orleans for medical treatment, advanced Johnston to brigadier general and, in January 1837, gave Johnston command of the entire army. But in the meantime, Felix Huston, who had been elected major general by the malcontents, had assumed command of the army, and he wasn't about to give up his command to the upstart newcomer Johnston.

With both men refusing to back down, the dilemma between Johnston and Huston could be resolved only by a duel. After several shots were fired by both men, Huston won the duel by shooting Johnston in the hip. For a while it was a popular victory for Huston, but as later sentiment began to swing toward Johnston, Huston left the army. Johnston gradually recovered from his wound, and in early 1838 he became Secretary of War in the Republic of Texas under President Mirabeau B. Lamar.

After Texas joined the Union, Johnston re-entered the United States Army and achieved distinctions as a general. Then came the secession of the South and the Civil War. As a general in the Confederate army, Johnston became a hero of the South. He was killed at the Battle of Shiloh in 1862 and was buried at New Orleans. After the war, influential Texans, remembering his earlier service to their state, determined to bring his body to Texas and reinter it with honor in the Texas State Cemetery in Austin.

Plans were made to bring Johnston's body to Texas through Galveston, but Union General Charles Griffin refused to approve an elaborate funeral procession in Galveston. Appealing to General Philip Sheridan, Griffin's superior officer, the Texans received a further rebuff. In his response, Sheridan wrote: "I have too much regard for the memory of the brave men who died to preserve our Government to authorize Confederate demonstrations over the remains of anyone who attempted to destroy it."

The outraged citizens of Galveston held their funeral procession anyway, with thousands of men and women marching behind the hearse as it moved through the city. Promised federal intervention did not materialize. At the next stop in Houston, similar demonstrations were defiantly held. Houses

Profile of Albert Sidney Johnston grave at Texas State Cemetery

Photo courtesy of G. U. Hubbard Collection

were draped with streamers, and for two days mourners visited the coffin. Pictures of Robert E. Lee, Stonewall Jackson, and Jefferson Davis were prominently displayed. A long procession followed the coffin to the train that was to take it to Austin. One of the newspapers reported: "The bells are tolling. The solemn cortege is one mile in length. Five hundred ladies and little girls are on foot in the procession." Again, there was no federal intervention.

Johnston's remains were laid to final rest in the State Cemetery in Austin following similar demonstrations of respect in that city. In 1901 the Texas Legislature appropriated $10,000 for a suitable monument to be sculpted by Elizabet Ney and for a protective canopy over the grave.

Reference:

June Rayfield Welch, *People and Places in the Texas Past* (Dallas: G. L. A. Press, 1974).

Decimus et Ultimus Barziza Was as Noteworthy as His Name

It may be thought that Decimus et Ultimus was a rather unusual name to give to anyone. Having already used up all their fine family names, Ignatius Barziza and his wife were at a loss as to what to name their newborn son. After listening to Ignatius lamenting his plight, a friend asked, "How many have you had already?"

"Nine."

"Is this a boy or a girl?"

"Boy."

"Then, damn it all, Barziza, name him Decimus et Ultimus, and make it so!"

And so it was done.

Descended from Virginian aristocracy, Decimus had an impressive ancestral heritage. On his mother's side, England's Samuel Boswell and Ben Johnson were close friends of earlier generations, and in America, Thomas Jefferson and Benjamin Franklin were among friends of later generations. George Washington, Light Horse Harry Lee, the Byrds, and the Burrs were Virginian relatives. The surname, Barziza, derives from Venetian aristocracy.

After graduating from William and Mary College in Williamsburg, Virginia, in 1857, Decimus et Ultimus (Tenth and Last) migrated to Texas where, despite his name, he became a leading and influential citizen. Decimus fought as a Confederate soldier in the Civil War and rose to the rank of captain in Hood's Brigade. Wounded at Manassas and again at Gettysburg, Decimus was captured by the Union forces at Gettysburg and dispatched to a prison camp aboard a train loaded with prisoners. Jumping from the window of the moving train, he made his way to Canada, to Nova Scotia, to Bermuda, and finally back to Texas, where he was received as a hero.

Back in Texas, Decimus obtained a law degree at Baylor University and then went into politics. Becoming a leader in the Texas Democratic Party, he was elected to the state legislature from Harris County, and he played a major role in resolving the Coke-Davis gubernatorial dispute in 1874.

Richard Coke had been elected governor of Texas, but the incumbent governor, Edmund J. Davis, refused to acknowledge the validity of the election and refused to vacate the governor's office. Barricaded with armed guards on the lower floor of the capitol building, Davis was unapproachable. Decimus managed to establish communications with Davis and convinced him to let Decimus and a committee examine the election returns. The examination revealed Coke to be the true winner, and a joint session of the House and Senate met that afternoon and inaugurated Coke.

Decimus also led a minority movement to block a bill granting an illegal extension of time to the Texas and Pacific Railroad for complying with the requirements for a land grant. Speaking against the bill on the floor of the House, Decimus vowed to block the vote by continuing to speak until adjournment time. Being forced by the sergeant-at-arms to resume his seat, Decimus and others resigned from the legislature. Leaving politics, Decimus began the practice of law.

Eloquent at pleading cases, Decimus became in great demand as a criminal lawyer. According to his nephew, Philip Dorsey Barziza, "Uncle Dessie" was so eloquent and convincing in one case that the prosecutor withdrew and the jury acquitted the accused without even leaving the jury box.

It was customary for the lawyers to gather at a bar or in a private home following the trials to celebrate their victories or drown their sorrows if defeated. Decimus participated in these gatherings with enthusiasm, and his wife frequently resorted to sending young Philip as the only means of getting him to come home. Philip would come in and say, "Uncle Dessie, it is time to go home." The invariable reply would be, "All right, little man, let's go."

Decimus et Ultimus died at his home in Houston in 1882 at the age of forty-three following a lingering illness. On his headstone in Glenwood Cemetery is the following inscription:

"Although his career was brief, he was distinguished among his fellow men as a gallant soldier, a wise legislator, and a brilliant and learned lawyer. He possessed in the highest degree the grand qualities of human nature: Honor, Genius, and Enthusiasm." His portrait hangs in the Jury Assembly Room in the Harris County Civil Courts Building in Houston.

Reference:

R. Henderson Shuffler, "Decimus et Ultimus Barziza," *The Southwestern Historical Quarterly*, April 1963.

The Spindletop Oil Field Confounds the Experts

It wasn't such a big hill, only about fifteen feet high. But the area known as the Big Hill in Beaumont was destined to become very big in importance.

One day Pattillo Higgins took his Sunday school class on a picnic to the Big Hill. Sticking his cane into the spongy soil, he entertained the children by setting fire to gasses escaping from the hole made by the cane. A student of geology, Higgins became convinced that oil lay beneath the surface.

In 1892 Higgins and some friends organized the Gladys City Oil, Gas, and Manufacturing Company and let out contracts for drilling two wells. In Higgins' mind, oil would be found about 1,000 feet down, and he protested that the drilling equipment to be used was too light to go that deep. Nevertheless, the contractors went to work, but before attaining even 500 feet in depth, they became discouraged and gave up. Higgins quit the company while retaining some of his leases on the Big Hill.

Bringing an assistant state geologist to the Big Hill to assess the possibilities, Higgins was told that there was no possibility of oil there. Local people began to ridicule him, calling him "the millionaire."

Portrait of Pattillo Higgins at Spindletop Museum

Photo courtesy of G. U. Hubbard Collection

163

Portrait of Anthony Lucas at
Spindletop Museum

*Photo courtesy of G. U. Hubbard
Collection*

Now seeking investors
from across the nation, the
undaunted Higgins got one
reply to an advertisement he
had placed in an engineering
journal. An Austrian, Antonio
Luchich, who had migrated to
America and had changed his
name to Anthony Lucas, sent
Higgins a positive response.
Lucas, a mining engineer,
wanted to drill. After entering
into a contract with Higgins, Lucas began drilling, but again,
the equipment was too light. However, he did find a small quan-
tity of crude oil before abandoning the hole. Lucas then
persuaded the Standard Oil Company to examine the area, and
after visiting the site, Standard's chief geologist proclaimed,
"You will never find oil here."

The only encouragement came from a University of Texas
geologist who put Lucas in touch with James Guffey and John
Galey, who agreed to help finance another well. Lucas leased as
much of the area as possible, and Galey marked a spot near
some sulphur-water vats into which farmers dipped their hogs
to cure mange and kill fleas. A drilling company consisting of
three Hamill brothers was hired, and the drilling began.

At 1,020 feet it appeared that no progress was being made.
Pulling the bit and drill stem, the Hamills attached a new bit to
the stem, and as they were lowering it down into the hole, a
deafening roar began. Then all of a sudden the well blew in
with the fury of a volcano. Scattering for safety, the workers
watched as mud spurted high up into the derrick, shattering the
drill stem, and then as they approached the well again, mud,
gas, and finally oil shot 200 feet into the air. Lucas shouted, "A
geyser of oil! A geyser of oil!" The time was 10:30 A.M. on

January 9, 1901. Returning that afternoon from a trip, Pattillo Higgins was not at all surprised. "For ten years, this is what I've been telling you would happen." So powerful was the erupting oil that ten days were required for Lucas to place a valve on the shaft and bring the flow under control.

Beaumont became a boom town overnight. Within weeks, the population mushroomed from 9,000 to 50,000. Land prices went from $20 an acre to $50,000. Sleeping accommodations were unavailable for latecomers. Some men bought 30-day

The Spindletop gusher transformed the world

Photo courtesy of Tyrrell Historical Library, Beaumont, Texas

Pullman tickets so they could sleep on the night trains from Beaumont to Houston and back.

The Lucas-Higgins well on the Big Hill produced more than twice as much oil as all of Pennsylvania, which until that point was the nation's leading oil-producing state. After the next five gushers were drilled, the new oil field was outproducing all the rest of the world.

Named Spindletop because of a tall cypress tree that had been compared to an inverted spindle, the new oil field ushered in the nation's first oil boomtown and initiated a revolution in fuel oil and transportation that changed the world.

References:

June Rayfield Welch, *People and Places in the Texas Past* (Dallas: G. L. A. Press, 1974).

Rex Z. Howard, *Texas Guidebook* (Amarillo: The F. M. McCarty Company, 1970).

Conrad Hilton Got His Start in Cisco, Texas

Conrad Hilton wanted to be an entrepreneur. He wanted to own a chain of banks. The question was where and how to start. While visiting a friend in Albuquerque in 1919, the friend advised Hilton to go to Texas. World War I had just ended, and Texas was experiencing oil booms at Burkburnett and Ranger. Oil and money were flowing freely.

Heeding his friend's advice, Hilton went to Wichita Falls, but the banks there were not for sale at any price. He went to Breckenridge and experienced the same result. Finally he found himself stepping off a train at Cisco, a small West Texas town not far from Ranger. Walking across the street to the first bank he saw, Hilton found that it was for sale. The owner in Kansas City was offering it for $75,000. After examining the bank's books and determining that the bank was well worth the price, Hilton wired an acceptance of the owner's price. When the reply came back from Kansas City, the telegram read: "Price up to $80,000 and skip the haggling."

Hilton was mad. He had accepted the owner's original price without any haggling, and now this response. "Tell the man he can keep his bank," Hilton shouted to the telegrapher, and he strode across Cisco's main street to a two-story red brick

The Mobley Hotel, which became the first Hilton Hotel

Photo courtesy of G. U. Hubbard Collection

A restored bedroom in Hilton's first hotel

Photo courtesy of G. U. Hubbard Collection

building, the Mobley Hotel. Hilton wanted a room in which to rest and think things over.

The Mobley's lobby was filled with people clamoring for rooms, and before Hilton could make his way to the registration desk, the manager closed his book and shouted, "Full Up." There was not a room available for Conrad Hilton. After the crowd had dispersed, the manager came up to Hilton, who was leaning against a pillar, and accused him of loitering. Now Hilton was really mad. He couldn't buy a bank, and he couldn't even get a room. A conversation ensued, however, in which Hilton learned that the hotel was so busy that rooms were rented for only eight hours at a time and they were always full for all three eight-hour shifts. That sounded to him like a good business opportunity. Learning that the manager was also the owner, Hilton asked if the hotel was for sale.

"Fifty thousand cash and a man could have the whole shooting match including my bed for the night."

"Mister, you've found yourself a buyer," Hilton responded.

"You don't get the bed till I get the cash."

Conrad Hilton's life and direction changed permanently at that point from banking to hotels. Gathering the necessary funds from several backers, he bought the hotel, and the rest is history.

One further anecdote, though in a more recent setting, is appropriate here. In 1955 Hilton opened the luxurious Beverly Hilton Hotel in Beverly Hills, California. He planned a gala opening celebration with screen stars, fanfare, and elegance,

167

and he very much wanted his sister, Felice, to attend. After receiving her invitation, Felice responded by postcard: "My dear Connie. It was nice of you to ask me to your party, but you have probably overlooked the fact that it is time to can peaches." It is nice to have one's priorities well defined.

Reference:

Conrad N. Hilton, *Be My Guest* (Englewood Cliffs: Prentice-Hall, Inc., 1957).

C. W. Post Revolutionized America's Eating Habits

While all people do some good during their lives, a few people bring about major changes that impact almost everyone. Charles W. Post was such a man.

Suffering from a nervous breakdown, Post came from Illinois to Fort Worth in 1886 hoping the change of climate would be beneficial. While in Fort Worth, he dabbled in real estate and helped establish the Sylvania Addition. Living on a 200-acre ranch in what is now Forest Park, Post maintained adequate health until 1890 when he suffered a relapse. Changing climates again, he entered a sanitarium in Battle Creek, Michigan. In charge of the sanitarium were Dr. John Kellogg, superintendent, and W. K. Kellogg, business manager, who were supplementing their patients' diets with food substitutes made from grain.

Because the coffee in the sanitarium was atrocious, Post decided that he also could devise a food substitute. He had known poor people in West Texas who produced better coffee than that in the sanitarium by mixing chicory with roasted wheat. Recovering sufficiently to leave the sanitarium, Post remained in Battle Creek, and after a period of experimentation, he developed a beverage from wheat, bran, and molasses. Post gave this new beverage the name of Postum.

Aided by an aggressive advertising strategy, Postum quickly caught on. The new beverage became such a success that a number of competitors arose, one of which was Monk's Brew, which was really the same thing as Postum but selling under a different name. Because Postum was selling at twenty-five cents and Monk's Brew at five cents, Post was feeling the competition. But rather than lowering the price of his Postum, Post bought out Monk's Brew. With Post controlling both ends of the price range, the other competitors quickly dropped out of the picture.

Then recalling the remaining packages of Monk's Brew, Post repackaged the product into Postum packages and easily sold them for twenty-five cents. Postum was now the unchallenged coffee substitute.

It turned out that Postum sales were greatest in the winter. Therefore, to fill the summer slump, Post developed Grape-Nuts in 1897. Another of Post's new cereals, Elijah's Manna did rather poorly until 1904 when Post changed its name to Post Toasties. Other cereals followed in quick succession. The General Mills Corporation emerged, and over the years dozens of food products were added to the General Mills family.

Following his retirement from General Mills in 1906, Post returned to Texas with his wife and daughter, and he again became a real estate developer, this time helping to develop Garza County in northwest Texas.

Until Post's arrival, Garza County had been administratively attached to Borden County for judicial purposes. Low rainfall and parched lands made farming and ranching difficult, and the population of Garza County was sparse. At a barbecue given on the OS Ranch to honor the Post family, Mr. Post made a speech in which he proposed that Garza County become reorganized for self-government. He also proposed establishing a model farm colony and a modern town. Because spring roundup was in progress on the OS, a large number of cowboys were present, and they welcomed Post's proposal with enthusiasm. They even took up a collection to help defray expenses for an election to be held early in 1907. The election was successfully petitioned, and after the votes were counted, the result was overwhelmingly in favor of independence from Borden County. It is said that even the horses voted in favor of the measure.

In 1907 Post also founded the town that bears his name. Post, Texas, situated at the foot of majestic Caprock escarpment, became (and still is) the county seat of the fully independent Garza County. It was known as Post City until its formal incorporation in 1914.

Post went to great efforts to help the residents of Garza County cope with the arid conditions that prevailed. Sponsoring new agricultural techniques that helped make farming profitable in that area, Post even made experiments in rainmaking.

Believing that upward air currents would condense atmospheric vapor and produce rain, he exploded many charges of dynamite, both in the air and on the ground. It is claimed that these experiments were 40 percent effective.

Although Post, who died in 1914, had created an empire in foods and had revolutionized America's eating habits, he was a Texan at heart.

References:

June Rayfield Welch, *People and Places in the Texas Past* (Dallas: G. L. A. Press, 1974).

1999 Texas State Highway Guide

Claude Dooley and Betty Dooley, *Why Stop? A Guide to Texas Historical Roadside Markers* (Houston: Gulf Publishing Company, 1985).

Did Jay Gould Place a Curse on Jefferson, Texas?

In the 1870s Jefferson was the metropolis of northeast Texas. Because of its navigational access through Caddo Lake and the Big Cypress Bayou to the Red River, Jefferson was a focal point for shipping. As such, it rivaled the Gulf coast port of Galveston. Jefferson, however, did not continue in its prosperity. Because the Big Cypress Bayou became too shallow for large vessels and because railroads began replacing water transport, Jefferson's role of prosperous eminence began to decline.

Visitors to Jefferson are treated to a grand story pertaining to the city's decline. It seems that Jay Gould, the great railroad tycoon, recognized Jefferson's potential. Coming to Jefferson at the end of 1881, Gould proposed building a railroad through the city, and he further proposed that the citizens of Jefferson raise the funds needed to finance the construction. Having purchased the Texas and Pacific Railroad in 1881, Gould was in a position to control its future development and routing.

Feeling prosperously secure with their river transportation, the city fathers refused Gould's proposal, thus sending the railroad tycoon into a rage. "Grass will grow in your streets, and

Jay Gould's private railway car at Jefferson
Photo courtesy of G. U. Hubbard Collection

bats will roost in your belfries," Gould supposedly proclaimed. Further, an entry in the guest register of the Excelsior House in Jefferson bears Gould's name along with an entry saying "end of Jefferson."

Although the story of Gould's visit is proudly recited by Jeffersonians, many historians dispute its authenticity. However, one fact in recent times stands out in support of the episode.

In 1954 it became known that one of Jay Gould's private railway cars was abandoned and sitting on a weed-infested track in Rusk County between Kilgore, Overton, and Henderson. The thirty-five women of the Jessie Allen Wise Garden Club in Jefferson decided that the car should be brought to Jefferson to be displayed as a fitting contradiction of Gould's prophecy of the extinction of the city. Determining the ownership of the car, the ladies purchased it for $1,500 and had it transported to Jefferson. Restored to its former grandeur, the car now serves as a museum and as a fitting reminder that Jefferson, although now a quiet rural community, survived in spite of Jay Gould's curse on the city.

Reference:

Fred Tarpley, *Jefferson: Riverport to the Southwest* (Austin: Eakin Press, 1983).

Social Life

Introduction

F rontier life was not "all work and no play." Recreation, religion, education, and social activities of various kinds were vital ingredients that enabled the colonists to maintain balance in their rather Spartan way of life and to stimulate their spiritual and intellectual needs.

Dances were especially popular forms of social recreation, and for the most part they were eagerly anticipated and attended by well-behaved participants. Religion was another important ingredient of frontier life. Some communities had their own minister, while others relied on the "circuit riders." Religion and dancing, however, did not always coexist harmoniously.

The social life also included picnics, hayrides, and ball games. There were quilting bees for the women and competitions of prowess among the men.

Education was important. Most communities established their own schools for the lower grades, and many communities also created academies offering high school and college-level instruction.

Eking out a living, coping with the vagaries of climatic conditions, and defending themselves against various forms of opposition required continual hard work and long hours. Still, the settlers made time for socializing and self-improvement.

When a Dance is Held in Your Honor, You Should Attend

Probably the most important social activity for both men and women on the frontier were the dances that were frequently held. As a partial compensation for the hardships and privations of frontier life, some recreation was needed, and the dances were well attended. They sometimes lasted all night. In Texas and Oklahoma, these dances seemed to be especially popular. Invitations were never sent out; word just circulated, and people came from miles around.

Music was usually furnished locally with whatever instruments were available. Adhering to unwritten dress codes, the ladies wore dresses with high necklines made of anything from silk to calico, and the men generally came in a coat with some kind of a tie and had their pants tucked into their high-top boots. Hats and guns had to be checked at the entrance to the dance hall.

Because the male population was much more numerous than the female, the male attendees were given numbers, and the floor manager would call out numbers identifying the men to participate in each dance. In this way participation was distributed equally and potential trouble was avoided. It was rare that a female sat out any of the dances, and whenever a large number of ladies were present, the dance was truly a special occasion.

On one occasion in No Man's Land (now the Oklahoma panhandle), it became known that a family named Dale was moving in from Missouri. The thing that made this family special was that John Dale had nine daughters, and several of them were of dancing age. Excitement spread through the ranks of eligible bachelors as they anticipated the arrival of this family of nine daughters.

"We'll have a dance to celebrate their arrival," they voiced in unison. "And we'll give those daughters a real welcome." Plans were made for the welcoming, and the dance was held on the night of the Dale family's arrival.

Now, another custom with frontier dances was that explicit invitations were never sent out. News of a dance spread naturally, and everyone came who wanted to come. All were welcome who behaved themselves, and people sometimes came from as far away as thirty or fifty miles. But the Dales did not know the frontier customs, and without explicit invitations to the dance, the Dale daughters not only did not attend, they went to bed early to rest from their arduous journey.

"Where are they?" the men at the dance asked.

"Maybe they think they are too good for us," one opined.

"We need to give them a real cowboy welcome," voiced another.

The Dales were all sleeping peacefully when suddenly they were awakened by pistol shots. Looking out their window, they saw cowboys riding around the house shooting and yelling like Comanches. The girls were thoroughly frightened, and they cried to their father to make the men leave. Wisely, John Dale did nothing, thinking that the riders would go away soon, which they did.

A few days later when everyone understood what had really happened and why, the cowboys became nice and friendly, and the Dale family was made to feel truly welcome.

Reference:

Carl Coke Rister, *No Man's Land* (Norman: University of Oklahoma Press, 1948).

Flour Sacks Made Excellent Frontier Underwear

Flour-sack underwear in Texas was probably just like flour-sack underwear anywhere else in the West during frontier times. The normal procedure was to bleach out the printing and then cut and sew the material to fit the body as needed. Frills such as tucks and ruffles were frequently added to give the female wearer a little more feeling of femininity.

A story from the Texas frontier shows the humor that sometimes creeps into such situations. Although the story is true, the lady's name has not been preserved, so let's just call her Jane.

Reared in Philadelphia where she had been trained for a musical career, Jane married a man named John and moved with him to Texas where they began a life of raising sheep. It was a rather severe adjustment for this Eastern-bred lady who had hardly washed a dish or mended a stocking before making the move. She enjoyed Texas, however, and relished the frontier life.

After two years in Texas, Jane's underwear began to wear out. Her dresses, made of good strong material, were holding up nicely, but the more delicate fabrics underneath were going to have to be replaced.

"John, do you think you could get me a few yards of white material at the store the next time you go to town?" she asked.

Although wanting to oblige, John explained that they barely had enough money for maintaining the sheep and that he had already borrowed more money than he felt good about. "Could you possibly wait until the wool is sold this fall?"

Jane later claimed she had not yet heard of flour-sack underwear, so when she decided to sew two flour sacks together to make a pair of drawers, she thought she was doing something ingenious and original. It turns out that Jane had

179

also never heard of methods for bleaching out the printing on the sacks.

She managed to make the drawers, complete with ruffles, tucks, and featherstitching, and she was very proud of the completed item. She could hardly wait for John to come in that evening so she could show off her handiwork. Dancing in front of him and twirling around as she lifted her skirt, she asked, "How do you like it?"

Breaking out in laughter, John could hardly control himself. Taken by surprise, Jane was more than a little bit hurt as her husband's laughter continued. When finally he regained his composure, he was able to tell her what he had seen. Quite visible on the rear of his wife's anatomy were large pink letters spelling out "THE PRIDE OF TEXAS."

Needless to say, Jane quickly learned the art of bleaching.

Reference:

Winifred Kupper, *The Golden Hoof* (New York: Alfred A. Knopf, Inc., 1945).

Dancing Was Considered by Some to Be a Tool of the Devil

Although dancing was a popular and well established social activity on the frontier, it was looked upon as a tool of Satan by many of the more conservative clergy. Children in families that frowned on dancing often found it difficult to stay at home while friends and neighbors were reveling in music and dance, and it was not at all uncommon for such children to sneak out of the house at night and listen to the music while concealed outside the home or building where a dance was being held.

In Lebanon, Texas, just south of Frisco, one old-timer expressed his feelings that "nothing ever took more joy out of the hearts of young men and women living in Lebanon during the 1890s than the attitude of the church fathers toward dancing." Many men were "churched" for dancing; i.e., they were brought before the church fathers and called to repentance.

One devoted church member was so caught up with joy and happiness on one occasion that he danced a jig on the front porch of the Lebanon barbershop. He had always danced jigs and had never felt that they were harmful. But on this occasion, he was summoned to a church court to answer for his sin.

"What prompted you to do such a thing?" they asked him.

"I was happy."

"Don't you know that dancing is an evil practice?"

"I accept that now, and I will never do it again."

"Are you sorry for what you have done?"

"I am sorry that I sinned, and I will never do it again. But I am not sorry for dancing a jig."

"You just talked yourself out of the church," the fathers pronounced.

181

Despite the attitudes of some of the clergy toward dancing, dances were the only source of social entertainment in many frontier communities, and they were well attended with jovial relationships and strict rules of proper conduct.

Reference:

"The Sinful Jig," *The History of Frisco* (Dallas: Taylor Publishing Company, 1976).

Frontier Medicine Was Primitive at Best

Qualified doctors were few and far between, and those few who were available had to know a little about everything. Specializations and modern medical practices as we now know them were nonexistent in those days. Not only were many of today's curative medicines not known then, but also anesthetics to deaden the pain of surgery were not available. Whiskey was one of the few effective painkillers and healers.

A few weeks before Sam Bass was killed in Round Rock in 1878, one of his men took a bullet wound in the leg. Passing all the way through the fleshy part of his thigh, the bullet left an open wound that had become infected, and gangrene was setting in. Some of Sam's men went for a doctor, and when he arrived in the outlaw camp and saw the situation, he immediately called for hot water. After washing the wound and applying antiseptics, the doctor told Bass that he needed to probe and clean the interior of the wound. From his pack, Bass pulled out some new silk handkerchiefs and handed them to the doctor who intended to soak them with antiseptic and pull them through the wound.

"Boys, those new handkerchiefs are going to be pulled through that bullet hole, hurt or no hurt," Bass explained to his men. "Now let a man get to each leg and arm and one to his head and hold him steady. No matter how much he hollers, hold him till the doctor says quit."

The men did their jobs as the doctor successfully cleaned the wound from one end to the other. The patient recovered.

In 1871 Cash McDonald and Green Freeman were wounded in a fight with Indians in Montague County. Knowing that killing the chief was the surest way to stop an Indian fight, Freeman did just that. But in the process, another Indian shot Freeman in the arm, severing the main artery. In the same melee, McDonald caught an arrow in his back. The two men were taken to the home of Cash McDonald's father in the community of Montague, but there was no doctor available there. So riders set out for Gainesville, about thirty-five miles to the east to summon the nearest doctor. Two days later Dr. Bailey and a young assistant arrived from Gainesville.

In the meantime, the bleeding in Freeman's arm was kept under control by a tourniquet that had to be loosened periodically to allow blood to circulate into the lower part of his arm. Someone pulled the arrow out of McDonald's back, but just the wood came out, leaving the steel spike embedded in a joint of the backbone.

Working first on Freeman, the doctors could not find the ends of the severed artery because it had shriveled and shrunk. They had to open the arm from the shoulder to the elbow, stretch the artery until the ends touched, and sew the ends together.

Next they instructed McDonald to sit on a chair facing the back of the chair. The other men were instructed to hold McDonald's arms and legs against the chair. Then taking a pair of blacksmith's tongs, Dr. Bailey probed for the spike, and after much tugging and pulling (and groans by McDonald), the doctor succeeded in extracting the spike. Freeman and McDonald both recovered and lived to enjoy old age.

Frontier medicine was primitive at best, but it accomplished miracles on numerous occasions. Medical techniques have come a long way in the last 150 years.

References:

Marvin F. London, *Indian Raids in Montague County* (St. Jo: S. J. T. Printers).

J. Frank Dobie, "The Robinhooding of Sam Bass," *True West*, July-August 1958.

The Men May Have Been Even Fussier About Their Looks Than Women

Although one tends to think of the western frontiersman as physically hardened and somewhat weatherbeaten (which was true when the men spent long periods of time in the fields or on the trail or in the mountains), a thorough restorative treatment in the local barbershop was very much a part of frontier life. The barbershop was an important retreat, not only for male fraternization and gossip, but also for restoring a weathered cranium to a more attractive visage.

In these more modern times, one now thinks of a barbershop as a place for a haircut and hairstyling. Not too many years back, the barbershop menu was haircut, shampoo, and shave. Styling was not yet in vogue. But on the frontier around the turn of the century, the barbershop could be a real tonsorial emporium. And no other area was ahead of Texas in terms of services offered. The barbershop at Spindletop during its boom days offers a typical example.

Cutting, of course, was the first order of business. After the cutting, singeing was one of the typical barbering services. Singeing was the process of burning the ends of a person's hair in order to retain the natural oil of the hair. Believing that the loss of natural oil would rob the hair of the necessary nutriments that facilitate its growth and development, barbers singed the hair of people "whose hair was of fine texture, inclined to brittleness and of sparing growth and density."

Shampooing, which was developed into a ritualistic art form, came next. With respect to shampooing, a 1912 *Barber's Journal* describes a typical visit to a barbershop at the turn of the century.

Having had his hair cut the way he wants it, the man then has a shampoo. There is the egg shampoo, the prepared egg shampoo, the tar shampoo, the patent preparation shampoo, and a combination of any of those shampoos. After a man has been shampooed, he is ready for the finishing touches.

Last but not least was the facial treatment—improving the coloring of the skin. There were treatments for skin having too little color, and there were other treatments for skin having too much color. Again from the 1912 *Barber's Journal*:

Suppose a man lacks color, his cheeks are white and have not that healthy peach bloom of the simple life. The barber rubs his cheeks with rouge or a liquid preparation and then colors them in this fashion. Suppose the mustache is not quite brilliant or stiff enough. The barber rubs it with a liquid preparation which makes it brilliant, stiff, bristly, and beautiful.

Suppose any part of the facial geography is too red. The barber treats the offending part with a liquid preparation which takes the color out of the skin. After all is attended, the man is released.

The frontier barbershop was truly a place where a man's vanity could be and was indulged.

Reference:

Spindletop Museum Barber Shop, Beaumont, Texas.

El Paso Became a Prizefighting Center of the World

Although it was a wide-open town in the latter 1800s, businessmen in El Paso felt that their town had become too dull in 1896. It needed enlivening that would attract nationwide publicity of a favorable kind.

In January 1896 a group of El Paso businessmen contacted Dan Stuart, an Eastern boxing promoter, and offered a $6,000 purse to stage a heavyweight championship fight between Bob Fitzsimmons, the American champion, and Peter Maher, the Irish champion. Accepting the proposition, Stuart even offered to put on a whole boxing carnival that would include championship bouts in other weight divisions with purses that would attract the best fighters. It was to be a gala occasion for El Paso. But prizefighting was not generally regarded as a respectable sport in those days, and people in other areas had other thoughts about the proposed carnival.

Calling a special session of the state legislature, Texas governor Charles Culberson got a bill passed prohibiting prizefighting within the borders of Texas. The territories of New

Arena erected for the Maher-Fitzsimmons fight

Photo courtesy of G. U. Hubbard Collection

Mexico and Arizona succeeded in getting a federal law passed prohibiting such fights in their areas. Even Mexico banned prizefighting, claiming it was more brutal than bullfighting. The clergy in El Paso were also in vigorous opposition to such degrading spectacles.

Despite all the mounting opposition, the promoters in El Paso were determined to go ahead, at least with the main event, but as the appointed time approached, a company of Texas Rangers under Captain Bill McDonald arrived to enforce the law. Mexico sent troops to protect its border from such desecration, and New Mexico had its national guard on the alert. It appeared for a while that there was no legal place in which to stage the fight. Then the promoters remembered a sandbar in the Rio Grande at Langtry where jurisdiction was unclear because Texas was not a nation at that time. Judge Roy Bean, who held court at Langtry, agreed to sponsor the fight.

Early on the morning of fight day, a special train carried spectators from El Paso down to Langtry for the main event. Fitzsimmons and Maher climbed into a hastily built ring on the sandbar while Texas Rangers and Mexican authorities squabbled over who had jurisdiction. But at fight time, both groups were numbered among the spectators. Although the fight succeeded in attracting nationwide attention, it lasted only eighty seconds. It ended with Maher lying flat on his back and Fitzsimmons virtually untouched.

As a side note to this affair, the pre-fight activities made quite an impression on a certain boy in El Paso. While young Louis "Jack" Hubbard was out playing in the yard, his next-door neighbor, Mr. Floyd Paine, drove up with a rather large man in his carriage. Calling to the boy, Paine said, "Jack, I want you to meet Bob Fitzsimmons, the heavyweight champion of the world."

"There he was," Jack later wrote, "towering above me, over six feet tall, sandy-haired, with a lot of freckles on his face, tremendously broad shoulders, long arms and big hands. I could hardly believe my eyes."

The champion bent down, taking the boy's small hand in his big fist, and said, "It's an honor to know you, my son."

Hubbard stood speechless as Fitzsimmons and Paine went into the latter's house. This was a treasured memory that small boy fondly carried with him throughout his long life.

Reference:

Louis H. Hubbard, "A Boy's Impression of El Paso in the 1890s," *Password*, Fall 1966.

Cowboy Boots Are Here to Stay

Cowboy boots were the most prized and expensive part of a cowboy's wardrobe. They were just as important to the cowboy as his Stetson hat. Although the first boots on the range were cast-off Civil War uniform boots, the true cowboy boot came quickly after the war.

The first cowboy boots were a combination of the American cavalry type and the British Wellington. Made in Coffeyville, Kansas, the boots were tall, coming almost to the knee to protect the cowboy's legs when he was riding. Tall boots also protected the cowboy from spiders and rattlesnakes when he was on the ground, and they made it more difficult for sand and gravel to bounce into the boot. These first boots were tight as well as tall. It is believed by some that because cowboys did so much riding rather than walking, their feet did not grow to the size of modern-day standards, and being vain about their small feet, the cowboys liked their boots tight. Initially, boot sizes ranged from four to nine; today they go from eight to eighteen. The tightness also helped them keep their balance while in the saddle. Patterns of stitching were sewn into the upper leather of the boots to stiffen them and keep the upper part from flopping over or bunching up around the ankles. The heels were the width of the boot and were relatively short and flat. To make these tall, tight boots easier to pull on, straps known as mule-ears were sewn into the uppers to give the cowboy something with which to tug.

Over the years the boots evolved into today's styles. As cowboys began to wear chaps, there was no need for the boots to be so high. Decorative stitching was added. Pointed or rounded toes provided greater comfort and stability. The heels became narrow and tapered and up to two inches high. This made the boots more adaptable to the saddle stirrups but also less uncomfortable for walking. Frequently, if a cowboy was thrown from his horse and had to walk home, he took his boots off for walking.

Although there are now many boot makers, the Justin boot became known as the "Standard of the West." In 1879 H. L. "Joe" Justin made his way from Indiana to Spanish Fort, Texas. Being near where the Chisholm Trail crossed the Red River, Spanish Fort became a favorite watering hole for cowboys before making the crossing. Although Justin was working in a barbershop, he had had some prior experience as a cobbler.

Soon after Justin's arrival in Spanish Fort, a cowboy, O. C. Cato, manager of the XIT Montana ranch, asked Justin to make him a pair of boots. "I'm on my way to Dodge City," Cato said, "and I'll get them on my way back." Being pleased with the result, Cato later suggested that if Justin could devise a way of taking a cowboy's foot measurements, Cato could sell boots for him. Justin's wife, Annie, designed a paper for tracing foot measurements and a tape for measuring the ball of the foot and the heel. These kits were used successfully, and Joe Justin became the first commercial maker of cowboy boots.

Justin's business was booming, and when the railroad reached Nocona in 1888, he moved the business there to make shipping easier. Joe would rise at 4:00 each morning and start working. When Annie had breakfast ready, she would signal Joe by putting a lighted kerosene lamp in the window.

Joe and Annie had six sons and one daughter. In 1908 Joe took his sons into the business, and in 1925, seven years after Joe's death, the sons moved the business to Ft. Worth.

Not wanting to go to Ft. Worth, Joe's daughter, Enid, remained in Nocona where she borrowed some money and established her own boot manufacturing company, the successful Nocona Boot Company. Enid married twice, with each marriage ending in divorce. Because each of her ex-husbands opened his own boot company, one of Enid's brothers suggested that she not marry again as she was creating too much competition for the family business.

Enid was a salty woman known as being "tough as a boot." She would walk through ice and snow if the weather was too bad to drive to work. Her business thrived, but finally, when her health began to fail, she merged it with that of her brothers.

There is now a Justin Industries, Inc., which owns the Justin, Nocona, and Tony Lama boot companies.

Cowboys today are quite different from what they were in the past. Although they still ride horses, they also travel in jeeps, pickup trucks, and helicopters. Nevertheless, it seems that cowboy boots are here to stay.

Reference:

M. Jean Greenlaw, "The Evolution of the Cowboy Boot," *Texas Studies Annual*, 1955.

Early Texans Were Hard on Mormon Missionaries

From its beginning in 1830, The Church of Jesus Christ of Latter-day Saints (commonly known as the Mormons) was an evangelical group. Missionaries went in all four directions and into all parts of the world, attracting thousands of converts to this new religion. But because of unsavory reports regarding Mormon beliefs and practices, the missionaries encountered great difficulties in some areas such as Texas. Many people were unable to listen objectively to the spiritual message the missionaries sought to convey because of a widespread fear that the ultimate aim of the missionary work was to recruit wives and daughters to come to Utah to augment polygamous relationships.

Morris J. Snedaker was a missionary in southeast Texas in the mid-1850s, and although he succeeded in getting his message across and winning several converts, this thirty-seven-year-old missionary also encountered severe persecution.

On one occasion in Gonzales, Texas, some twenty-five or thirty men with faces painted black drug Snedaker from a home owned by a Mr. Lindsley. Dragging him barefooted over stones and prickly pears, they exhibited him at several houses before bringing him back to the starting point. At each house the dogs would come out barking as though they were ready to eat the prisoner, but the mob made such a racket yelling and horn blowing and bell ringing that the dogs would scurry back under the house and hide.

Back at the Lindsley home, the mob saddled Snedaker's horse and ordered him to mount it, but being weak from exhaustion, Snedaker dropped to the ground. He later recorded in his diary: "They caught me by the feet and jerked me along for a number of rods over the rough ground with my head and shoulders thrashing upon the ground saying, 'You heretic, you ought to be killed.'"

Finally getting Snedaker onto his horse, the mob took him to other homes for further display. This activity continued until dawn when they stopped, tied him to a tree, and began beating him and spitting tobacco juice on him. Then putting him back on his horse, the mob ordered him to leave and not be seen in those parts again. As Snedaker was about to ride off, one of the mob struck him with a club.

"After I had started, one of those princes came with a club nine or ten feet in length and gave a blow that would have straightened me prostrate upon the ground had not the club broken in three pieces. It knocked me blind though I succeeded in sticking upon my horse."

Upon completing his mission in other parts of southeast Texas, Snedaker returned to Salt Lake City where he became the first manufacturer of domestic salt from the Great Salt Lake. He died in 1882, just four days shy of his sixty-fourth birthday.

Reference:

Norman B. Ferris, "The Diary of Morris J. Snedaker, 1855-1856," *The Southwestern Historical Quarterly*, April 1963.

Some Duels Had Unexpected Outcomes

For many years in America, as well as in other nations, duels were an accepted means of settling disputes or restoring honor among individuals. But in some cases the duels resulted in unexpected outcomes. Noah Smithwick, in his book *The Evolution of a State*, tells of one such duel in which he had a role. In Stephen F. Austin's colony community of San Felipe, a Mr. Moore and a Mr. McKinstry had a falling out and decided that the only honorable recourse was to settle the matter by dueling. Each man came to Smithwick to be trained.

The method of training was to attach a tape at a man's height to a tree and have the duelist-in-training shoot at it. Moore proved consistent in his aim, and his bullets cut the tape more often than they missed. On the other hand, McKinstry never hit the tape and quite often missed the tree entirely. Smithwick was certain as to who would be the victor, and if the opportunity had presented itself, he would have bet money on it.

The appointed day for the duel arrived and the two contestants lined up, strode their paces, turned, and fired. Sharpshooter Moore missed entirely, while McKinstry's shot hit Moore just above the ankles, breaking both legs.

It was an entirely unexpected result. Discussing the duel later with Jesse Thompson, Smithwick expressed his surprise. How could Moore be so accurate when shooting at the tree but not in the real duel. Thompson had a good explanation. "Ah," he said, "the tree had no pistol pointed at Moore when he was shooting at it."

Indeed, experience in all walks of life bear out the truism that while practice is absolutely necessary, mental preparation is a vital ingredient in preparing for difficult assignments.

Reference:

Noah Smithwick, *The Evolution of a State* (Austin: The University of Texas Press, 1984).

Grayson College
Had Strict Standards

Education was important to the settlers of the West who were far removed from eastern educational opportunities, and small colleges and academies sprang up in many western locales. Founded in 1880 at Whitewright, Grayson County, Texas, Grayson College was one such institution.

Besides offering college courses and being accredited in the late 1880s by the University of Texas, the college also maintained a primary and high school. This arrangement worked well and made the college eligible for state funds as a "free school." But it also enabled some former students who had not finished the third grade to claim the distinction of being ex-students of Grayson College.

In 1893 the college was flourishing to the point that it outgrew its small campus, and a new three-story brick building was built on a new campus. Peak enrollment at the college occurred in 1904 when 840 students attended.

While maintaining high academic standards, Grayson College differed from many other colleges of those times in that it was co-educational, and at times the schoolmaster was severely taxed in maintaining "proper" discipline among the students. The following set of rules was adopted and published in the college's 1888-89 catalog.

1. No profane or other indecent language shall be used on or about the college grounds.
2. No pupil shall cut, mark, scratch or otherwise injure or deface the building or furniture.
3. No pupil shall, by word or deed, insinuate the slightest disrespect to teachers.
4. Pupils shall not loiter around business houses, depots, hotels, or other places in town.
5. All pupils are required to be present and stand the monthly examinations in their respective studies.

6. Students shall not attend balls, hops, or parties.
7. No young man shall engage any young lady's company at home or as an escort elsewhere; nor shall they walk or talk with each other to or from the college or on the streets at other times; nor shall they have, at any time, any written communication through the mail, from the date of entrance to close of the session.
8. Pupils from a distance will be under the care of the Presidents and of the landlord and landlady of their boarding house; they must comply with such regulations as their boarding house may have.
9. In monthly written examinations, pupils shall make at least 75%, or be dropped to a lower grade, provided they fall below 75% any two consecutive months.
10. If at any intermediate or final examination a pupil should fail to make 75%, he will be compelled to review the course.

These rules, especially Rule #7, may seem to be quite restrictive by today's standards, but they were quite acceptable in the late 1800s.

During the college's peak enrollment year of 1904, a fire destroyed the three-story building. Although other buildings were constructed as replacements, the college never fully recovered from the disaster. Enrollment continually declined until 1912 when the college closed its doors and ceased to exist.

Reference:

Emory Christian, "Grayson College," *History of Grayson County Texas*, Vol. II (Tulsa: Heritage Publishing Company, 1981).

Frisco's Commercial Hotel
Was the Place to Stay and Eat

If anyone wanted a good meal back in the early 1900s, the Commercial Hotel in Frisco, Texas, was the place to be. Lunch, including drink and dessert, was fifty cents for all you could eat. An overnight room was only $1.50 with breakfast or lunch included.

In 1917 a work crew building a telegraph line spent several days at the Commercial Hotel where Mr. Woodall and his crew thoroughly enjoyed the food. As the line pushed southward, the crew moved on to Carrollton about fifteen miles down the line. But two days later, Mr. Woodall and his crew were back at the Commercial. "The food is better here," they said.

Each morning the men traveled from Frisco down to Carrollton to work and then back to the Commercial at night. And each day they sent a man on a railroad handcar back to Frisco to pick up their lunch.

They say that an army travels on its stomach. So did a certain telegraph line building crew.

Reference:

Mrs. Bessie Burks Sprouse, "Commercial Hotel," *The History of Frisco* (Dallas: Taylor Publishing Company, 1976).

Orphan Trains Bring Needed Help to the Frontier

The Reverend Charles Loring Brace had a revolutionary idea. Troubled by the large numbers of orphans and abandoned babies in New York City and other eastern cities, this Methodist minister, who had founded the Children's Aid Society of New York, reasoned that many of the problems of caring for these homeless youths in the East could be alleviated by sending them to the western frontier where young and strong bodies were needed for field labor and household chores. In the late 1800s the nuns in New York's Foundling Hospital were finding as many as 1,000 abandoned babies on their doorstep every year, and caring for them properly until their adult years was an impossible task. After their few years of infancy, Brace reasoned, these children could be loved and would be useful to many families out West. Thus the Reverend Brace conceived the idea of shipping these youths by train to western settlements for adoption by frontier families.

These trains, known as "orphan trains," went almost everywhere from Minnesota down to Texas, and from the 1850s to 1929, as many as 350,000 children made the trip. Stopping in rural areas, the arrivals of these trains were heralded major events in America's westward migration.

"We'd stop in these little towns and get out of the trains, and they'd interview us," recalled Stanley Cornell in retrospect. "It was kind of like a cattle auction. If they liked us, they'd take us." Cornell and his brother, Victor, rode the trains twice before being "taken" by a family in Wellington, Texas. Having two daughters and no sons, the man wanted and needed some boys. When Stanley (age 6) and his brother (age 5) passed the interview, which consisted only of "Do you like farms and animals?", the man gave them a bag of jelly beans and took them home.

As an alternative to begging for food in an orphanage with 600 other children, the orphan trains were a sweet second chance for many and a nightmare to others. As might be expected, life with their new families brought mixed reactions. Dorothy Sharpley recalls being rejected by her first adoptive family. "I was sent back to New York only to ride the train again. My mother loved me, but all my father cared about was how much farm work I could do."

Stanley and Victor Cornell had a similar experience. Taken in by a family in Coffeyville, Kansas, on their first trip, Stanley remembered that "they were kind and we liked them, but after a couple of months they sent us back. I still don't know why." Their subsequent adoption in Wellington, Texas, turned out to be a happy and permanent arrangement.

Today only a scant few orphan train riders are still alive. Six of them attended a reunion recently in Lakewood, Colorado, and relived that adventuresome and traumatic period of their lives.

Reference:

Robert Weller, "Riders of Orphan Trains Reunited," *Denton Record-Chronicle*, April 30, 2000.

God Help the Fish Down Below

Sam Houston, statesman, politician, soldier, and general patriot, also had his dark side. Although gifted with wisdom, oratory, and persuasiveness, this hero of Texas in its formative years was not given to outward displays of religion or spirituality. So when he met and courted Margaret Moffette Lea, to whom religion was vital, the irresistible force met the immovable object. For many years it was quite a contest as to which one was the more irresistible and which was the less immovable.

Houston, who in earlier years had lived with the Cherokee Indians and who had had an Indian wife, met Margaret in May 1839 in Mobile, Alabama. The forty-six-year-old Houston had come to Mobile to discuss real estate with Margaret's mother who was looking for investment opportunities in Texas. Although Houston's visit was for business purposes, he spent enough time with Margaret to propose to her before leaving Mobile. Nancy, Margaret's mother, opposed the union of her daughter to a man so much older than Margaret and so steeped in the ways of the world. But when it appeared that the marriage would take place anyway, Nancy sat down with Houston and read him Biblical passages that she thought he should know.

Because of an urgent need to return home, Houston tried to persuade Margaret to come to Texas with him and be married there, but she would not agree to a wedding anywhere but in her hometown of Marion, Alabama. So on May 7, 1840, Houston arrived in Marion by stagecoach, and the couple were married two days later. When asked why she had chosen a man such as Sam Houston, Margaret said, "He had won my heart." Even so, she was intent on reforming Houston's hard drinking habits and on making him one of God's disciples.

Following the wedding, the couple traveled to Texas where Margaret spent the rest of her life. Although the marriage,

201

which produced eight children, can be termed successful, Margaret continually tried to persuade Sam to spend less time in politics and more time with her. As president, governor, and senator, Sam Houston spent more time away from home than at home. Margaret finally succeeded in reforming her husband of his drinking, but she never succeeded in weaning him away from politics. Preferring to remain in the background, Margaret endured many lonely days and weeks. Yet, the two were devoted to one another.

Primarily because of Houston's political activities, he and his family resided in several locations such as Austin, Galveston, Independence, and Huntsville. Everywhere they went, Margaret associated herself with the Baptist church, but although she urged Sam to attend church meetings with her, he was not a churchgoer. Nor was he inclined to submit to baptism despite Margaret's continual urging that he needed to save his soul. In his mind baptism was for full believers, and Sam had too many questions and negative opinions about organized religion.

At Independence, Margaret became one of the organizers of the new Concord Baptist Church, and there her desires for her husband's baptism were finally realized. On the occasion of a series of revival meetings, Dr. George W. Baines, a prominent Baptist minister, approached the Houston home on horseback, and Margaret, determined that this was the time, stopped Baines with the plea that he talk to her husband.

"He has the greatest confidence in your knowledge of such things," she told him.

The next morning Houston and Baines rode into Brenham together and discussed religion along the way. Sam was particularly troubled about a passage in Corinthians to the effect that church members who partook of communion unworthily would "seal their damnation forever." He had no desire to make such a "sad and awful mistake." Baines explained that the passage referred, not to those who are trying to live righteously, but to those who succumbed to feasting and drinking to satisfy animal yearnings and thereby mocked holy symbols. Sam thought the matter over, accepted Baines explanation, then announced to Margaret that he was ready to be baptized.

The baptism ceremony was arranged and scheduled to be performed in a special baptistry carved out of limestone in the shape of a coffin in the bed of Kontz Creek, north of Independence. But when the party arrived there on the appointed day, they found that some mischievous boys had filled the baptistry with mud and tree limbs. The party had to move to Little Rocky Creek where the local minister, Dr. Rufus Burleson, performed the ceremony by immersing Houston in the creek's cold waters on November 19, 1854.

It is reported that shortly after the baptism, Burleson commented to Houston: "Well General, all your sins have been washed away."

"If that be the case," Houston replied, "God help the fish down below."

On his deathbed on July 26, 1863, Houston's last words were said to be: "Texas... Margaret—Margaret." Margaret, who was in poor health much of her later life, died of yellow fever four years later in Independence.

References:

James M. Day, "Margaret Moffette Lea Houston," *Women of Texas* (Waco: Texian Press, 1972).

June Rayfield Welch, "Houston Was Baptized at Independence Church," *Historic Sites of Texas* (Dallas: G. L. A. Press, 1972).

Mrs. Georgia J. Burleson, *The Life and Writings of Rufus C. Burleson* (1901).

Madge Thornall Roberts, *Star of Destiny: The Private Life of Sam and Margaret Houston* (Denton: University of North Texas Press, 1993).

William Seale, *Sam Houston's Wife: A Biography of Margaret Lea Houston* (Norman: University of Oklahoma Press, 1970).

William Carey Crane, *Life and Select Literary Remains of Sam Houston of Texas* (Freeport, N.Y.: Books for Libraries Press, 1972).

Places

205

Introduction

N ames and locations of towns were matters of vital importance on the frontier.

Many neighboring communities found themselves in competition with one another for the coveted role of county seat, and trickery and subterfuge were often used to sway the decision. There were also vigorous competitions among rival towns to lure the railroads and their attendant commercial advantages, or to gain access to a needed natural resource such as water. Some towns bypassed by the railroads actually relocated themselves. Securing a rail line through a town meant survival and prosperity.

Town names, some of which are unique, were also subjects of serious consideration. While many names were chosen to honor heroes, past or present, or to repeat place names from a former locale, some town names were politically motivated, and a few were simply the result of the light-heartedness often experienced after periods of extreme effort. (On the frontier, there were many periods of extreme effort.) Oftentimes, railroad officials named towns to honor themselves or their employees.

Behind each place name there is a story, and in many cases the stories are quite amusing.

Where the Texas Archives Go, the Capital Goes

In 1839 Austin became the capital of the newly formed Republic of Texas, and as an independent nation the Texas government established a repository in Austin for its "national archives," state papers, and records of land titles. However, in March 1842 when a Mexican army seized San Antonio, critical concerns arose regarding the location of the capital and the safety of the archives. With the enemy so close to Austin, many residents and government officials fled the city in what was called "the breakup."

President Sam Houston ordered the archives buried, which was done by a local "Archives Committee." Houston also moved the government first to Houston and then to Washington-on-the-Brazos, despite vigorous opposition by the majority of Austinites. Because of the threat imposed by the near proximity of the Mexican army, Houston felt this was the right time to accomplish the move, and he felt that if he could get the archives out of Austin, the rest of the government would naturally follow. To accomplish the transfer, twenty-six men arrived secretly in Austin on December 29, 1842, and in the darkness of night began loading the archives on wagons. But they hadn't reckoned on encountering Mrs. Angelina Eberly.

Mrs. Eberly firing a cannon in the Archives War

Photo courtesy of Texas State Library & Archives Commission

A noted innkeeper in Austin, Mrs. Eberly was one of the few women remaining in Austin during the breakup, and she was a fervent and spirited supporter of keeping the capital in her city. Finding the men loading the official papers in the darkness, she sounded the alarm throughout the community. Mrs. Eberly then raced down to the city's cannon at Congress Avenue and Pecan (now 6th) Street, and she managed to fire it at the departing wagons. About twenty-six men quickly formed an unofficial posse and rode off in pursuit of the wagons, hauling a cannon from the local arsenal with them. Some twenty miles out of Austin, the posse caught the wagons and retrieved the coveted archives without bloodshed.

Although the archives stayed in Austin, President Houston and the Texas Congress remained in Washington-on-the-Brazos, the temporary seat of government. Finally, in 1845, during the presidency of Anson Jones when Texas considered the American offer of annexation, the Texas Congress returned to Austin to once again make that city the permanent capital.

Reference:

Claude Dooley and Betty Dooley, *Why Stop? A Guide to Texas Historical Roadside Markers* (Houston: Gulf Publishing Company, 1985).

Quanah Becomes the County Seat of Hardeman County

Before 1890 the small community of Margaret served as the county seat of Hardeman County, Texas. But residents of Quanah wanted to have the county seat and subsequently found a unique law that worked in their favor.

Margaret, at that time, was larger than Quanah and had more males of voting age. Thus the citizens of Margaret thought they could easily outvote the citizens of Quanah if ever the question of moving the county seat should appear on a ballot. But Quanah found a way to add to its list of voters.

The Fort Worth and Denver Railroad had just built through Quanah on its way northward, and there was a law along the railroad that if a man had his washing done in a town for six consecutive weeks, he thereby could be counted a citizen of that town. So the citizens of Quanah went into the laundry business. By the time election day came on February 10, 1890, every FW&D railroad employee between Fort Worth and Texline on the Texas-New Mexico border was a qualified citizen of Quanah and a certified voter. On election day three Quanah saloons added incentives by keeping open house and offering

Quanah Parker monument at Quanah

Photo courtesy of G. U. Hubbard Collection

209

free drinks to any man who voted "right" as long as he could take them standing.

The Hardeman County Commissioners Court records show that Quanah received 688 votes compared to 164 for Margaret and one for Chillicothe. Thus Quanah became, and still is, the county seat of Hardeman County, Texas.

———————————

Reference:

The Medicine Mound Gazette, printed at Quanah, Texas.

Crazy Water or Crazy People?

Although mineral springs and health spas abound throughout the country and the world, there are none that quite matched the mystique of the Crazy Water wells that gave birth to the city of Mineral Wells, about fifty miles west of Fort Worth. It is likely that the aura of the name was just as responsible for the success of the area as was the curative power of the waters.

It all started back in 1877 when the James Alvis Lynch family moved to the area from their farm near Denison, Texas. Both Mr. and Mrs. Lynch were severely plagued by rheumatism, and most of the family suffered also from malaria. Seeking a higher and drier climate, they traveled in a westerly direction, and on Christmas Eve, they pitched camp a few miles east of the Brazos River where Mineral Wells is now located.

Water at the Lynch's new location was scarce. Early attempts to drill water wells failed, and Lynch hauled water to the camp from the Brazos River. Finally a well driller came along in July 1880 with the right equipment, and he succeeded in drilling down to the water table. But the water tasted funny and smelled bad. The Lynch's sixteen-year-old son took the first drink of the new water, and when the others saw that it did not hurt him, they also began to sample the liquid. After drinking the water for some time, Mrs. Lynch's rheumatism subsided and

The Crazy Hotel is now a home for senior citizens

Photo courtesy of G. U. Hubbard Collection

she became able once again to carry on the normal duties of wife and mother. Mr. Lynch's rheumatism also vanished.

Word of the water's curative powers spread quickly, and people began flocking by the hundreds to this newly discovered "fountain of youth." By 1881 as many as a thousand people could be found camped on the Lynch farm seeking cures. Lynch sold tickets for five cents each that entitled the bearer to one quart of water per day. Judge Lynch, as he became known, also laid out the town of Mineral Wells and sold lots to new arrivals.

Many additional wells were drilled, and one well drilled by W. H. "Uncle Billy" Wiggins was responsible for the name that became attached to the water. Unfortunately, there are several versions of the story. In one version, two women who were suffering from hysterical mania caused by severe feminine disorders drank the Wiggins water and regained their sanity. In another version, a woman afflicted with epilepsy would have a seizure whenever she drank the water. The most common version is that a woman who had withdrawn from the world could always be seen sitting near the Wiggins well, and school children began referring to her as the crazy woman. Regardless of how it came about, the Wiggins well began to be known as the Crazy Woman Well.

The name stuck, and it became almost a byword throughout the country. Railroads built into Mineral Wells. The Crazy Water Bottling Company was established, and Crazy Water Crystals became popular throughout the country. The large Crazy Hotel was built, complete with baths and massages as well as Crazy Water for drinking. Next, the towering Baker Hotel was built, and people from around the world flocked to Mineral Wells.

Site of the first crazy water well at Mineral Wells

Photo courtesy of G. U. Hubbard Collection

Besides being a restorative spa, the city became a social center for the wealthy and the elite, and the hotel registers were graced with the names of millionaires from the East and movie stars from the West.

Although over 200 wells were drilled, the boom is over now, and most of the wells are capped. The two large hotel buildings are still there and are serving as retirement homes for the elderly. But in its heyday, Mineral Wells was the place to be.

Reference:

Gene Fowler, *Crazy Water* (Fort Worth: Texas Christian University Press, 1991).

Some Texas Place Names Have Their Own Special Stories

Every state has towns and cities bearing unique and interesting names. While it may be a challenge to top such names as Slippery Rock, Pennsylvania, or Truth and Consequences, New Mexico, Texas is not lagging when it comes to interesting names.

There are interesting derivations of many place names, and also some rather bad jokes about some of Texas's place names. Texans consider it fortunate that Sour Lake (in southeast Texas) is so far removed from Sweetwater (in West Texas). Although Rising Star (in Eastland County) and Sundown (in Hockley County) are both in West Texas, you shouldn't try to see Rising Star until you have seen Sundown first. And it seems strange that Salt Flat is closer to Sweetwater than to Sour Lake, while Sugar Land is closer to Sour Lake than to Sweetwater.

The curative waters of Sour Lake were long used by the Indians. Recognizing the lake's potential for attracting health seekers, the early settlers built a large health resort with baths that became a favorite spa for Sam Houston among others.

Many of the streams around Sweetwater are tainted by the area's gypsum deposits. The water in Sweetwater Creek was sweet by comparison and provided the only potable water for the early settlers.

The town was very naturally named for the life-sustaining sweet waters.

City limit sign at Dime Box
Photo courtesy of G. U. Hubbard Collection

214

The citizens of Rising Star originally chose Star as the name of their community, but the U.S. Postal Department rejected the name because there was already a Texas town with that name. After arguing all night about a different name, the naming committee adjourned, and as they started home they looked up and saw Venus, the morning star. The rising star of Venus brought unanimity to the committee, and Rising Star became the name of their community.

Round Rock, just north of Austin is named for a relatively flat and round rock in the middle of Brushy Creek, which marked a low water crossing for Spaniards, Mexicans, Indians, and Texans. Hundred-year-old wagon wheel ruts may still be seen in the creek bottom.

The name of Muleshoe, in West Texas, derives from a mule shoe found by a family moving to the area from Dodge City, Kansas. Considering the shoe a good luck piece, they not only saved it but also used it to brand their cattle as they amassed a large and profitable ranch.

Bigfoot, Texas, in Frio County southwest of San Antonio, was named for William A. A. "Bigfoot" Wallace, one of the more colorful characters in early Texas.

Texas has other towns with unusual names, like Cut and Shoot located between Conroe and Houston, but perhaps the most unusual situation of all was the town that literally remained nameless. Surveyed in the 1850s and populated in 1868, a small community took root in Travis County near Austin. In 1880 the townspeople applied for a post office. After recommending six names for the community and having the postal authorities reject all six names, the citizens disgustedly decided: "Let the post office be Nameless and be d____d." The postal authorities accepted the suggestion, and the town had an official name: Nameless.

First known as Browne's Mills, Dime Box, Texas, in Lee County was located in Stephen F. Austin's "Old Three Hundred" colony. Mail for Browne's Mill kept getting mixed up with mail for Brownsville. When the postal authorities requested a change from the former name, the townspeople chose to call their post office "Dime Box" as a token of their long-standing practice of dropping dimes into the mill's mailbox as a tip for postman

John W. Ratliff, who traveled weekly into Giddings, the county seat, to deposit outgoing mail and procure incoming mail. When the Southern Pacific railroad built to within three miles of Dime Box, a portion of the town was moved to the tracks. Thus, today there is an Old Dime Box and a New Dime Box.

Several other Texas towns have undergone name changes for rather unusual reasons. The name of San Angelo, while not an unusual name, has an interesting derivation. This southwest Texas town was originally named Santa Angela in honor of a Mother Superior of the Ursuline Convent in San Antonio. Popular usage shortened the name to San Angela, and this is the name submitted to the postal authorities for the town's post office. But because of the mixture of San (masculine) and Angela (feminine), the postal authorities rejected the proposed name. Angela was then changed to Angelo, and the resulting name was adopted.

About thirty miles east of Austin, the city of Bastrop has had two name changes. When founded in 1832, the town was named Bastrop in honor of Philip Hendrik Nering Bogel, Baron de Bastrop, who had helped Stephen F. Austin obtain the grant for the first American colony in Texas.

Over the next two years, the Mexican government developed serious doubts about the loyalty of the Texians to Mexico, and in April 1834 Stephen F. Austin was languishing in a Mexican jail under suspicion of working for the annexation of Texas to the United States. Something had to be done to demonstrate the Texians' allegiance. As one means of placating Mexico, Oliver Jones, a close friend of Austin, proposed to the legislature of Coahuila and Texas that the town of Bastrop be renamed Mina. Francisco Xavier Mina was a national hero and martyr in Mexico, and the name change was intended as one means of convincing the Mexican government of the allegiance of the Texians to Mexico. The name change became official on April 24, 1834. Following the defeat of Mexico at the Battle of San Jacinto in April 1836, Texas became independent and there was no further need of placating the Mexicans, and Mina became Bastrop again.

Dime Box memorial
Photo courtesy of G. U. Hubbard Collection

Then there is Texarkana, straddling the Texas-Arkansas border and about thirty-five miles from both Louisiana and Oklahoma. Intended to be a marketing and distribution center for the four corners area, Texarkana is a compound of the names of the four states it serves. "Tex" comes from the first part of Texas, "ark" from the first part of Arkansas, "a" from the last part of Oklahoma, and "na" from the last part of Louisiana.

Texas is a colorful state in many ways, and some of its place names add much to its color.

References:

1999 Texas State Highway Guide

AAA Texas Tour Book

Claude Dooley and Betty Dooley, *Why Stop? A Guide to Texas Historical Roadside Markers* (Houston: Gulf Publishing Company, 1985).

B. W. Aston and Donathan Taylor, *Along the Texas Forts Trail* (Denton: University of North Texas Press, 1997).

John Holmes Jenkins III, Ed., *Recollections of Early Texas* (Austin: University of Texas Press, 1997).

Bolivar, Texas, Owes Its Name to a Mug of Rum

Bolivar, Texas, is one of those rural crossroads communities you pass through en route to somewhere else. Yet, Bolivar's residents, many of whom are descendants of the community's founders, are fiercely proud of the community's heritage. Located in the northwest portion of Denton County, Bolivar claims to have been the first settlement west of Collin County. As the first fort in Denton County, Bolivar was a bustling community in the 1840s. Two stagecoach lines changed horses there. Three hotels and several stores graced the town along with a cotton gin, a flour mill, a sawmill, a blacksmith shop, a saloon, a church, and a school.

Bolivar became an important center of the Texas cattle industry. It was near here that the Texas cattle trail joined the Jesse Chisholm Trail for the cattle drives up to Kansas. It was also here that the Texas cattle baron John Chisum kept huge

herds from which he supplied beef to the Confederacy during the Civil War. In later years Bolivar and the surrounding area became a haven for Sam Bass and his gang.

Plaque with bust of Simón Bolívar, donated to Bolivar, Texas, by the Venezuelan government
Photo courtesy of G. U. Hubbard Collection

218

When the fledgling community was first being settled, a controversy arose over the name by which it would be called. The preacher, who also doubled as the doctor, wanted New Prospect to be the name of the community, but another man who had migrated from Bolivar, Tennessee, argued for Bolivar as the name to be adopted. The controversy became a heated contest between the two proponents, and although it appeared for a time that the preacher would prevail, the matter became hopelessly deadlocked.

Finally an election was called to settle the issue once and for all. The town would be named New Providence or Bolivar, and the citizens would decide. The preacher, because of his spiritual and medical influence in the community, was sure his choice would prevail. But the man from Tennessee knew a thing or two about human nature, and he promised a mug of rum to every man who would vote for Bolivar. Bolivar was the overwhelming choice of the voters.

Indirectly it can be said that Bolivar, Texas, was named for Simón Bolívar, the great Venezuelan patriot. Actually it was named for Bolivar, Tennessee, which in turn was named for Simón Bolívar. At the crossroads of Bolivar, Texas, there is a prominent brass plaque donated by the country of Venezuela. The plaque commemorates the Texas town named after the Venezuelan hero, and it contains a bas-relief portrait of Simón Bolívar. Perhaps the plaque should also depict a mug of rum to symbolize the true source of the town's name.

Reference:

Texas State Highway Marker at Bolivar, Texas.

Boracho, Texas, Was Aptly Named

The Southern Pacific Railroad (from Houston and San Antonio) and the Texas and Pacific Railroad (from Dallas and Ft. Worth) were racing each other to be the first to build into Sierra Blanca in West Texas. It was a race of vital importance, as the winner would be awarded the right to build on into El Paso.

As they approached to within sixty-five miles of Sierra Blanca, the two railroads were making equal progress until heavy rains deluged the Southern Pacific route and brought construction to a virtual crawl. The route yet to be traversed became a veritable swamp, equipment bogged down in the sticky mud, and the situation appeared hopeless. Although the Texas and Pacific work crews also experienced rain, they were not affected nearly as much as the Southern Pacific workers. It appeared that the Texas and Pacific would easily win the race into Sierra Blanca. Then a strange thing happened.

One night, three tarpaulin-covered wagons mysteriously appeared in the Texas and Pacific work camp. Being curious, the T&P workers lifted the tarps and found the wagons loaded with cases and cases of tequila, whiskey, and wine. Being tired and somewhat bored in that desert wasteland, the workers decided it would be all right to have a small sip of the refreshing liquid so providentially provided. One sip naturally led to another, and when the sun came up, the workers were in no mood or condition to do any work. The cases were not yet emptied, and the party continued. In fact, a week went by with virtually no work accomplished before the men were sober enough to resume normal construction. But by that time, the Southern Pacific crews had slogged through their mud and were well on their way to Sierra Blanca. Needless to say, the Southern Pacific won the race and the right to build on to El Paso.

A small out-of-the-way town sprang up sixty-five miles east of Sierra Blanca on the site of the T&P party. Appropriately, the town promoters adopted the name of Boracho for their new community. Borracho is the Spanish word for drunk.

Reference:

Thomas P. Ramirez, "The Town Named After a Binge," *True West*, November-December 1960.

Characters Among the Populace

Introduction

A nywhere that a large number of people are to be found, interesting characters can be expected to be included. This is especially true among the kinds of people attracted to the Texas frontier by its opportunities and challenges. Settlers who excelled in all phases of frontier life could be found throughout America's frontier, and Texas was second to none in attracting unique and outstanding characters.

The colonists and settlers came from all walks of life. There were planters, woodsmen, cowboys, entrepreneurs, industrialists, fighters, outlaws, gamblers, healers, charlatans, and plain humbugs. Although many of the immigrants were colorful characters on an individual basis, the blend of their individual traits produced an invigorated populace that accomplished wonders.

Jacob Brodbeck Was an Early Pioneer of Air Travel

Credit for the first successful powered flight of a heavier-than-air craft has been awarded to the Wright Brothers for their experiment at Kitty Hawk in 1903. Also recognized is a brief earlier flight by Professor Samuel Pierpont Langley in 1896. But it seems to have been forgotten that a German-born Texan named Jacob Brodbeck preceded both the Wrights and Langley by making a similar flight just outside of San Antonio in 1865.

A quiet little schoolmaster, Brodbeck was a dreamer and an inventor. Before leaving Germany, he designed a clock that supposedly would run without winding. After arriving in Texas, he assuaged his fascination with the challenge of air-borne transportation by designing a man-sized airplane. Brodbeck's design used partly movable wings, a rudder, an enclosed cockpit, and a screw propeller powered by a clock-like coil spring.

Brodbeck built a succession of models and successfully demonstrated them at county fairs in San Antonio, Fredericksburg, New Braunfels, and other surrounding communities. In so doing, he succeeded in attracting financial backers for his full-scale experiment. The principal backer was a Dr. Ferdinand Herff, a wealthy physician who gained local fame by being the first doctor in San Antonio to use ether in his surgical procedures.

Completing his "man-sized" plane late in 1865, Brodbeck, his backers, and a large crowd of curiosity seekers gathered in a meadow outside of San Antonio. After readying his craft, Brodbeck gave the signal, and the plane left the ground, soared to the treetops, and then crashed. The plane was wrecked, Brodbeck was injured, and the confidence of his backers was permanently destroyed. Brodbeck had assumed that the coil

225

spring that powered the propeller could be rewound in flight by the pilot. He learned that it could not.

After recovering from his injuries, Brodbeck made many speeches throughout the United States trying to generate interest in his design, but without success. He finally retired to a farm near Fredericksburg where he lived out his remaining days.

Reference:

"Gillespie County and Fredericksburg, Texas," mimeographed document from the Fredericksburg Information Bureau.

Bigfoot Wallace Was Colorful and Active on the Texas Frontier

"Bigfoot" Wallace was a Texas hero with a reputation as big as his feet. Born William Alexander Anderson Wallace in Virginia, Wallace made his way to Galveston in 1837 at the age of twenty. His intent was to fight the Mexicans and avenge the deaths of his brother and a cousin who had been among those massacred by the Mexicans at Goliad.

Although the war had ended before Wallace's arrival, he remained and became every inch a Texan. Throughout his colorful life, Wallace, who was quite a large man, engaged in a variety of activities, and wherever he went, he was usually the center of attention in his various exploits.

Spending a brief time in San Antonio in 1838, Wallace observed the untouched ruins of the Alamo and the skeletal remains of some of the defenders that still lay in the ashes of the funeral pyre. Wallace's next stop was in Austin, which in 1839 became the new capital of the Republic of Texas, where a multitude of opportunities beckoned.

Bigfoot Wallace

*Photo courtesy of
Western History Collections,
University of Oklahoma Libraries*

227

At Austin, Wallace hewed logs for the new government buildings. Because threats of Indian attacks still existed, hewers were scarce, and Wallace received the princely sum of $200 a month for his work. Wallace then turned to the hunting and selling of meat. His smokehouse and the open front shack in which he lived with a friend, William Fox, were located at what is now 103 Rio Grande, just a few blocks west of present-day Congress Avenue. On almost any day, one could see Wallace's latest catches—buffalo, wild turkey, bear, deer, or wild cattle—tied to tree limbs on the grounds. Somewhat unorthodox in his methods, Wallace was once seen chasing a small herd of buffalo down the lane that later became Congress Avenue. The buffalo escaped by swimming the Colorado River at the foot of the lane.

Wallace also dug Austin's first water well, not for a home, but for a saloon keeper. He also helped haul building stones to Austin from the hills to the west of the new city. On one occasion, Wallace took refuge in a cave on Austin's Mount Bonnell to recover from a malady. Because he remained there longer than expected, the girl he was hoping to marry gave up on him and eloped with someone else.

Moving on from Austin, Wallace engaged in additional exploits. After Mexico's 1842 invasion of San Antonio, Wallace was among a force of Texans that pursued the withdrawing invaders into Mexico. The pursuing Texans were forced to surrender to the Mexicans following a battle at the Mexican town of Mier, and as the captives were being marched toward Mexico City, they attempted an escape at the Hacienda Salado. As retribution, one-tenth of the Texans were sentenced to die. The re-captured Texans were forced to draw beans from a jar. The seventeen who drew black beans were executed, those drawing white beans remained prisoners and were eventually set free. Wallace was lucky enough to draw a white bean.

One of the more popular stories about Bigfoot Wallace has to do with hickory nuts. One morning, Wallace awoke to find that Comanches had stolen all his horses except one named White Bean, which Wallace had staked in a different location from the others. On White Bean, Wallace had no difficulty following the Indians' trail that showed clearly on ground softened by recent rains. About mid-morning he found the Indians, forty-two of them, still in camp with his horses. Their camp was in a large stand of hickory trees, and it was that time of year when the ground was covered with hickory nuts. It was a golden opportunity for an unconventional man like Wallace.

Tying his shirt sleeve cuffs about his wrists and the bottoms of his pants about his ankles, Wallace scooped up hickory nuts and poured them into his otherwise loose-fitting clothing. Continuing until his clothing was filled with hickory nuts, he encased himself in armor almost as effectively as knights of merry England. His appearance, however, was that of a fat and lumpy scarecrow.

Creeping up to the Indians' encampment, Wallace felled two Indians with shots and then stood there while the startled Indians shot arrow after arrow at him. Their arrows were right on the mark, but the hickory-nut-shielding prevented their penetration, and they fell harmlessly at Wallace's feet. Very quickly the Indians determined that they were facing an invincible creature from another world, and they left in great haste. Recovering his horses, Wallace was back home before dark with a lot of cracked nuts for his hogs to eat.

There are two conflicting accounts of how Wallace acquired the nickname of "Bigfoot." In one account, the tracks of a large Waco Indian who had robbed a settler led to the cabin that Wallace and Fox were sharing. Following the tracks, the settler accosted Wallace and accused him of having committed the crime. As the tracks were those of a very big man wearing moccasins, and as Wallace, who also wore moccasins, stood six feet two inches tall and weighed 240 pounds, the settler's accusation appeared to be well placed. Wallace finally proved his innocence by putting his own feet into the Indian's tracks and showing that his feet were slightly shorter than those of the Indian.

In the other account, Wallace's feet matched the Indian's in size, and Wallace subsequently found and killed the Indian.

Both accounts agree that Wallace was a large man. And in either case, the incident prompted Fox to start referring to Wallace as "Bigfoot," and the nickname endured throughout Wallace's life.

References:

June Rayfield Welch, *People and Places in the Texas Past* (Dallas: G. L. A. Press, 1974).

Claude Dooley and Betty Dooley, *Why Stop? A Guide to Texas Historical Roadside Markers* (Houston: Gulf Publishing Company, 1985).

Rex Z. Howard, *Texas Guidebook* (Amarillo: The F. M. McCarty Company, 1970).

J. Frank Dobie, *Tales of Old Texas* (Austin: University of Texas Press, 1955).

James Elliot Was a Very Eccentric Quaker

James Elliot was probably the most eccentric man ever to arrive in the Quaker community of Friendswood. Unheralded and unknown, he arrived by foot in 1896, and he stayed until he died thirty-five years later. Elliot had a college education, and he had been a Quaker leader. But something had gone wrong in his life, leaving him harmless but mentally deranged.

Elliot's first stop was at the home of James Brown, Friendswood's founder, where he sought temporary lodging. Following supper, he said, "I am somewhat wearied by my long journey and I will retire, if thee will show me where I may sleep." The next day Elliot announced that he wanted to buy two hundred acres of land and plant potatoes. Learning that the visitor had no money, the Browns placed him in a little shack near their house, and there he stayed, doing occasional chores in return for food.

Elliot's appearance was as strange as his personality. His hair, which he never cut, hung in ringlets on his shoulders. He had a long, full beard and piercing black eyes. On his feet he wore high-topped shoes that were too big because one time he had split his right foot open cutting wood with an axe. To keep the soles from wearing out, he nailed horseshoes to each shoe. You could always hear him clomping down one of the oyster shell roads.

When his clothes wore out, he clothed himself with flour sacks and gunnysacks held together by safety pins. Even when he dressed for church, he often had a row of safety pins down the front of his black, frock-tailed coat. Instead of wearing a belt, he used a long rope wrapped around him in a certain way to serve both as belt and suspenders. One time when a newcomer took pity on Elliot and offered to buy him some new clothes, Elliot took the well-meaning person to his shack and showed him suit after suit stored in a trunk. "My brother sends me these," he explained.

Perceiving that Elliot was harmless, the residents of Friendswood accepted him and tried to help him. On land rented for him by a family named Harvey, he raised rice for a while and then onions. One time when working the land, he hitched one of the Harvey's milk cows to a log and whipped her when she wouldn't pull. When Mrs. Harvey saw what was happening, she came running and gave Elliot a good tongue-lashing. "Don't you ever again try to drive one of my milk cows."

Elliot loved children and delighted in helping them with their schoolwork. One time when the math teacher was having trouble with a problem, he sent one of the boys to fetch Elliot. "Read me the problem," Elliot said as he sat down in an old wooden chair. Instructing the teacher as to what to write on the blackboard, Elliot then said, "There is your answer, and there is the proof of it." At other times he was called upon to translate Latin into English, which he did with no difficulty at all.

One Thanksgiving Day, Russell Davis called on James Elliot with some food sent by Mrs. Davis. Russell found Elliot asleep on four straight-back chairs, covered with gunnysacks and with three cats sleeping on top of him. As Elliot began to stir, Russell said, "It's Thanksgiving Day, and my mother sent over your dinner."

"Well three cheers for the Davises," he shouted.

Elliot's eating habits were strange indeed. On another occasion, a kind matron brought him a large slice of dewberry pie. He dropped it into his bucket of sour milk and bread. From a birthday dinner, another friend brought him a plate of ice cream. This he also dropped into the bucket. Then from a bottle of quinine, he dropped his daily dose into the bucket and stirred the mixture. After everyone had gone, he ate his meal.

Elliot attended church every week. On cold winter nights he would clomp in carrying a kerosene lantern and clomp over to the pot-bellied stove to warm himself before sitting in a pew. Pushing his dirty black hat forward over his forehead, he would soon be fast asleep. Then all of a sudden he would wake up and pray. Russell Davis remembered that the man would "pray a prayer that was the most beautifully worded prayer I've ever heard from anybody. At times when he prayed he sounded like he was talking face to face with God."

Often in Sunday school, after some discussion, Elliot would rise to his feet and say, "Now I just want to explain this so the children will understand it." He would then launch into a discourse of technical theology laced with long words, delivering an explanation that no one could understand.

No one ever heard James Elliot say a bad word about anyone, and he never used slang in his speech. Despite his peculiarities, he was well liked by his fellow Quakers. In retrospect, Russell Davis said this of the man: "James Elliot was different from any man I've ever met; but when it comes right down to it, I liked James as well as any I've ever met."

References:

Friendswood Chamber of Commerce, *City of Friendswood: A Community Profile* (1992).

Joycina Day Baker, *Friendswood: A Settlement of Friendly Folks* (Austin: Nortex Press, 1994).

"Brick" Barnett Proposes Marriage

William Pomeroy "Brick" Barnett was in love. He was so much in love that he was willing to do almost anything if only Miss Ollie Hughes would become his wife. But how to propose? Brick Barnett did it by letter. His sentences conveyed his feelings quite clearly although his spelling left something to be desired.

Deer gurl

I hav bin thinin fur a gude while thet I wood rite you a leter
an tel you thet I wus luvin you beter eny uther gurl in texas
an ef you will mary me I wil be jist the bestest feller you
ever seed in the wurld I will fede the hoss an milk the cow
an slop the pig an chern the buter an eny theng else in the
wurld you tel me to. if you knode how much I luv you you
wood say yes when yuve thunk the mater overall tu your sef
I hope you will eny way. if you can luv me jist a little tenty
bit I wood fele awful gude if you wood tel me so the first
time you see me an ef you cante luv me donte luv thet uther
feller fur if you du it wood kill me deder an a dore nale to
no hit. fur I do kere fur you a ho lot, if not a lot, more. you
are the apple uf my eye.

Although Brick wrote additional paragraphs in his proposal letter, his opening paragraph quoted above was a poignant expression of his feelings for Miss Ollie. It was apparently well received, for the two were married on November 5, 1891, and they became the parents of eight children. The family attended the Methodist church in Whitesboro, Texas, where Brick was also a member of the Woodmen of the World (W.O.W.) and International Order of Odd Fellows (I.O.O.F.) lodges. He served as city marshal for twenty-five years.

Dying in 1933 at the age of sixty-four, Brick had lived a happy life because Miss Ollie was his beloved wife.

Reference:

Whitesboro Library, "Brick Barnett," *History of Grayson County Texas,* Vol. II (Tulsa: Heritage Publishing Company, 1981).

Uncle John Kerley: The Tightest Man in Town

John Kerley became a legend in Medicine Mound, Texas, for his miserly ways. Spending money unnecessarily was to him the greatest of all sins. As a result, Kerley became the subject of many an anecdote.

For example, Kerley, after much soul searching, went into Quanah in 1935 and bought a Ford car. Learning to drive, he took great pleasure in his new mode of transportation. For some reason he was especially sensitive about wearing out the brakes. So to minimize wear and tear on the brakes, he would conclude a drive by coasting into bales of hay lined up inside the barn. A year later when notified that he would have to pay $2.00 to renew the license, Kerley couldn't understand why he was being required to pay money to continue driving a car he already owned on roads that he also owned as a taxpayer. Refusing to pay the $2.00, he drove the car into the barn, put it up on blocks, and there it sat until the day he died.

Kerley and his wife were childless. Kerley preferred it that way as another mouth to feed meant additional expense. In the 1920s this outlook swayed Kerley's stand when he was showing his parsimonious ways regarding a proposed church donation to an orphanage at a time when "orphans' trains" were running through the Southwest. Orphans' trains were trains carrying orphans in need of adoption. Because the West was wide open and in need of people to work the land, trains loaded with orphans would leave large eastern cities and travel to the frontier areas. As the trains stopped in various towns according to advance advertisements, the orphans would be lined up on the station platforms for inspection by anyone interested in adopting them. A number of such orphans were adopted by Hardeman County settlers.

An elder in the local Church of Christ, John Kerley was the self-appointed guardian of the church's funds. As such, he was a lone voice in vigorously opposing a proposal to donate a sum of money to the Tipton Orphans' Home a few miles away in Oklahoma.

"Charity begins at home," he argued, adding that the money should stay at home and let other places take care of themselves.

Finally, one of the other elders spoke up and said, "Well, Uncle John, if that's what you really believe, I'll tell you what I'll do. Next time one of those orphans' trains comes through town, I'll take two orphans if you'll take one."

All of a sudden, the vote became unanimous for making the donation.

Reference:

Bill Neal, *Our Stories* (Austin: Nortex Press, 1997).

Don Pedro Jaramillo Heals the Sick

During the latter 1800s, a number of curative practices abounded throughout America. Patent medicine salesmen were numerous. Magnetic cures were popular. It became fashionable to drink and bathe in the many mineral water spas that proliferated. Along with these remedial practices, a few "healers" practiced their God-given skills. Don Pedro Jaramillo was such a healer throughout South Texas.

As the story goes, Don Pedro discovered his gift early in his life when he was moved upon to treat his injured nose with mud from a pond. After three days, the nose was completely healed. For the next twenty-five years, Don Pedro functioned as a healer.

Born in Guadalajara, Mexico, in 1829, Don Pedro made his way to Texas in 1881 and became a laborer on the Los Olmos Ranch just north of the present town of Falfurrias. Visiting the sick and ailing throughout South Texas, he ranged from Corpus Christi to Laredo to San Antonio. Upon returning to Los Olmos, he would sometimes be greeted by as many as 500 people seeking his help.

Don Pedro's prescribed procedures were varied according to the nature of the malady. He instructed some people to wear tomatoes or place garlic in their shoes. To others he prescribed doses of coffee or

Don Pedro Jaramillo

Photo courtesy of Western History Collections, University of Oklahoma Libraries

beer or whiskey to be taken over a period of days. An 1893 victim of sunstroke was instructed to go off by himself and bathe for nine successive days. He told a lady with heart trouble to drink a glass of river water five nights in a row. A woman with epilepsy claimed to have been cured by drinking a glass of water in her yard for nine straight nights. Such prescribed remedies are reminiscent of Elisha instructing Naaman to cure his leprosy by dipping himself in the River Jordan seven times (2 Kings 5:10).

According to the *San Antonio Daily Express*, Don Pedro treated the rich and poor, the silk dresses and the greasy blankets. There was no class distinction. The newspaper also reported that the best physicians of San Antonio visited Don Pedro on one occasion and came away "talking learnedly about hypnotism, mesmerism, and the faith cure."

Regardless of what one may think about the validity of such cures, Don Pedro had no shortage of testimonials from people claiming to have been cured by him. The physicians tried at one time to have the law shut Don Pedro down, but he was not breaking any law. He never accepted any payment or any other recompense for his services. Although he had once been arrested in Mexico on charges of being a wizard, there was nothing in his life that could be legally challenged.

According to Don Pedro himself, his was a gift of God, and it was available freely to anyone who sought his help.

Reference:

Gene Fowler, *Crazy Water* (Fort Worth: Texas Christian University Press, 1991).

Carry Nation Takes
Her Axe to Austin, Texas

At the turn of the century, Carry Nation, of Medicine Lodge, Kansas, waged a one-woman temperance campaign against the evils of alcohol and tobacco. Mrs. Nation, known as the Kansas Cyclone, traveled widely throughout the Midwest making speeches, smashing saloons with her axe, and trying to persuade men and women of sinful habits to a more temperate and moral life. Because she created such a spectacle wherever she went, Carry Nation always drew large crowds of curiosity seekers who wanted to hear her ranting and see her axe in action.

On October 16, 1902, Austin, Texas, joined the list of other cities that had "hosted" Carry Nation and her axe. As she stepped down from the train, "Uncle Tom" Murrah and a group of University of Texas students met her, and they proceeded at once to a saloon owned by Alderman Bill Davis at Congress Avenue and Fifth Street. Davis immediately ordered Carry to leave.

"Young man, do you know who you're talking to? I am Carry Nation, and I was never known to leave a saloon until I got good and ready."

"It makes no difference who you are," Davis responded. "One

Carry Nation tried to reform
the University of Texas

Photo courtesy of Western History Collections, University of Oklahoma Libraries

of us has to get out, and it won't be me."

Carry Nation swung her axe in Davis's direction. After ducking to avoid the blow, Davis grabbed Carry by the shoulders and pushed her out the door. Continuing her harangue on the street, Carry attempted to swing her axe again as the police arrived. Yielding to Murrah's pleas not to arrest her, the police allowed a hundred cheering students to escort Carry to the University campus. Not allowed to enter one of the halls, Carry began speaking from the steps to an enthusiastic crowd.

"Madam," cried a University official attempting to stop her, "we do not allow such."

"I am speaking for the good of the boys," she answered.

"We do not allow speaking on campus," he retorted.

"I have spoken to the students at Ann Arbor and at Yale, and I will speak to the boys of Texas."

With that, the crowd let out a loud yell of support that frightened the horse of a nearby postman. The bolting horse heaved the postman onto the ground and demolished his wagon against a tree, scattering letters and papers in all directions. Although the postman graciously declined Carry's offer to pay for the damage, she had lost the attention of the crowd and her attempt to resume her lecture was a futile effort. Leaving town the next day, Carry's reforms had not materialized, and her "boys" resumed their normal "evil" ways in peace.

References:

Carleton Beals, *Cyclone Carry* (Philadelphia: Chilton Co., 1962).

Robert Lewis Taylor, *Vessel of Wrath* (New York: The New American Library, 1966).

Did Judge Roy Bean Also Fight Bears?

In addition to being "the Law West of the Pecos," it appears that Judge Roy Bean may have engaged in other activities such as bear hunting.

Bean made frequent trips to San Antonio buying supplies for his operations at Langtry, Texas. On one such trip in 1884, Bean took time to visit with a friend, McClellan Shacklett, owner of a hotel and health spa a few miles south of San Antonio. As they spent the afternoon visiting and imbibing, Bean became more and more loquacious about his various exploits. Eventually the conversation turned to bears.

Recounting how he had killed seven bears in one afternoon, Bean recalled that after expending all his ammunition, another bear caught him and was squeezing him. Being unable to shoot, Bean told how he pulled out his Bowie knife and cut the bear to pieces.

Shacklett expressed his doubts, for having spent time in Bean's part of the country, Shacklett had never seen any bears out there, and further, he did not know anyone who ever claimed to have seen a bear out there.

Judge Roy Bean's pet bear

Photo courtesy of Western History Collections, University of Oklahoma Libraries

Nonplussed, Bean vowed that he was telling the honest truth. "When I get back, I'll send you a live bear as soon as I have time to go up into the hills and catch one."

One can imagine Shacklett's surprise a few weeks later as he stood on the grounds of his hotel-bathhouse and observed a railroad delivery wagon approaching with a cage on it. Inside the cage was a live bear. Accompanying the bear was a letter in which Bean described the harrowing experience of capturing the animal.

Shacklett became a believer until another of Judge Bean's friends saw and recognized the bear. The bear was a pet that Bean normally kept in his courtroom-saloon to entertain customers. Tame and ready to eat anything, the bear especially liked to drink beer out of bottles. Whenever trains stopped in Langtry, passengers would adjourn to the saloon where they would buy beer for the bear. With the bear consuming about ten bottles of beer every time a train stopped, Bean had a thriving business going.

With no use for a beer-guzzling bear at his health spa, Shacklett returned the bear to Judge Bean, and he still remained on the skeptical side about Bean's bear fighting exploits.

Reference:

Gene Fowler, *Crazy Water* (Fort Worth: Texas Christian University Press, 1991).

Diamond Bessie Creates a Sensation in Jefferson, Texas

When Abe Rothschild and Bessie Moore checked into the Brooks House hotel in Jefferson, Texas, on January 19, 1877, a melodrama began to unfold that would lead to the most famous murder trail in Jefferson's history.

Although the couple registered as "A. Monroe and wife," Abe was actually a member of a wealthy Rothschild family in Cincinnati and a distant relative of the European Rothschilds. His companion was a beautiful woman, scarcely in her twenties, with a checkered past. It is said that Bessie had been a prostitute, and that the couple had met in a house of ill repute. Although no record of their marriage has ever been found, they nevertheless became traveling companions, and they visited various cities together before making their way to Jefferson.

Bessie's beauty was enhanced by fine clothes and by the diamonds that she wore. With natural sunlight glittering from her adornments, Bessie caught the eye, and the envy, of all who observed her, and she soon became known in Jefferson as "Diamond Bessie Moore."

Portrait of Diamond Bessie in Jefferson's Excelsior Hotel

Photo courtesy of G. U. Hubbard Collection

On January 31, after residing at the Brooks House for almost two weeks, Abe and Bessie obtained picnic lunches on a warm morning, and they strolled toward the footbridge that crosses the Big Cypress Bayou. It was the last time they were ever seen together.

Returning alone to the hotel late that afternoon, Abe declined invitations for dinner, saying he had already eaten. When asked a day or two later about Bessie, he claimed she had gone to visit some friends, but would join him on Tuesday when they were scheduled to depart from Jefferson. On Tuesday morning their hotel room was found empty.

On February 5, while out looking for firewood, a lady named Sarah King came upon the body of a woman on an embankment just east of the Big Cypress ferry. She had met death from a bullet wound in the temple. The weather had been cold, with snow and sleet for several days, so there had been very little decomposition of the body, and there was no sure way of determining how long she had been dead. Although there were no diamonds present, people were sure that it was the body of Bessie Moore, and a manhunt began for Abe Rothschild.

The authorities located Abe in Cincinnati and sent him back to Jefferson to stand trial. In Cincinnati, he had become despondent and had tried to commit suicide by shooting himself in the head, but he only succeeded in putting out one eye and disfiguring himself.

In preparation for the trail, Abe's family, although they had disowned him, hired the best attorneys available for his defense. A team of nine attorneys, including U.S. Congressman David B. Culberson and his son, Charles A. Culberson, later Texas governor and U.S. Senator, collaborated on Abe's defense. Despite their efforts, Abe was convicted by his jury. Tradition says that the jury foreman, C. R. Weathersby, drew a picture of a noose on the wall of the jury room and declared, "That's my verdict." The other jurors signed their names under Weathersby's. Shortly thereafter, however, the conviction was nullified by an appeals judge on a technicality.

Another trial was held, and this time Abe was acquitted. One of the issues was that it was hard to believe that Bessie's body was in such a good state of preservation after supposedly lying in the open for five days. Immediately following the trial, some of Abe's family members whisked him out of the

Diamond Bessie's grave at Jefferson

Photo courtesy of G. U. Hubbard Collection

courtroom and onto a departing train. His subsequent fate is unknown.

Over the years Abe Rothschild has become regarded in Jefferson as a vile villain, while Diamond Bessie Moore has been accorded heroine status. Bessie is buried in the Oakwood Cemetery in Jefferson. A headstone was added in the 1930s by a retired foundry worker, E. B. McDonald, who acknowledged, "I placed it there one night because it did not seem right for Diamond Bessie to sleep in an unmarked grave." The Jessie Allen Wise Garden Club subsequently added an ornate iron fence. Bessie's grave is now one of Jefferson's tourist highlights.

Reference:

Fred Tarpley, *Jefferson: Riverport to the Southwest* (Austin: Eakin Press, 1983).

Animals

Introduction

Humans don't have a monopoly on intelligence. Indeed, the phrase "horse sense" is much more than a clever pair of words.

Various types of animals and various breeds within those types have inherent intellectual capabilities that make them especially adept at performing certain tasks. Wolves are clever hunters. Sheep dogs can be better shepherds than humans. An endless number of examples could be cited.

Occasionally, within these types and breeds, an individual critter will be blessed with seemingly special intelligence and understanding, thus making that critter especially useful, or adversarial, to man. Such natural intelligence in the animal world is both mystifying and awe inspiring.

In addition to natural intelligence, male animals aspire to leadership. Every herd or flock will have a natural leader that either assumed its position or attained it through battle. An animal that is a leader with special intelligence can be worth its weight in gold.

The Lobos Were Mean but Noble Animals

The lobo wolf, also called a timber wolf, is a fascinating animal. Although mean, the lobos also commanded the admiration and respect of those who knew them.

In earlier years, before their ranks were decimated by ranchers and bounty hunters, lobos traveled and hunted in packs, and they used clever strategies. Predetermining the course they wanted their intended victim to travel, pack members would station themselves at intervals along the course. A couple of lobos would then go into a herd, cut out the fattest animal, and drive it to the course that had been laid out. Charging down the course, the animal from the herd would quickly tire while fresh wolves, in a relay, were available to give chase. As the animal tired, the lobos would attack, first ripping open the rear flanks, and then opening the middle and disemboweling the dying animal.

In later years the lobos were reduced to hunting in families or alone. Rather than subjugating themselves to a pack mentality, the lone wolves exhibited their own personalities and wiliness. Some were more successful than others, and almost every sheepherder had his own stories about certain wolves that had evaded capture for years. Old Black, in the Big Bend area, did an estimated $30,000 of damage and was alleged to have killed two Mexican herders. Old Reddy, in Hays County, did $15,000 over a ten-year period. When finally captured, he was taken to the town square in San Marcos, Texas, and publicly executed.

A good lobo could survive for six or more years and kill up to $50,000 worth of sheep. A toll of thirty sheep in one night was sometimes achieved. Sometimes the lobo killed for food, sometimes just for sport.

The great reduction of the lobo population came as the result of concerted efforts by the ranchers. Sometimes the ranchers would go out on their own forays, and sometimes they would hire professional "wolfers" to do the job. On occasion it would take months to trap and kill a certain troublesome lobo. Each lobo had his own style of operation. "You can't catch every lobo by the same tricks," the wolfers would explain. Time was required to study the lobo's habits and learn where and when to expect his appearances. One of the tricks used by wolfers would be to capture a female lobo, spend a few months taming her, and when she was in heat, put her out as a lure for the killer lobo.

One significant trait of the lobos was that they rarely attacked humans. In Europe and Asia, wolves attack people, but in America they learned to stay away from the Indians arrows and spears and they transferred that same respect to the white men. Lobos might taunt, but they generally maintained a distance from the Indians and from the white men. When putting out a trap, every human sign and smell must be removed. Even when using a rabbit for bait, human smell must not be present. Lobos are smart and wary, and a human smell will cause them to leave everything alone.

In another way, wolfers were smart too. After displaying a lobo scalp to a rancher and collecting a bounty, the wolfers would ask to keep the scalp as a souvenir. They would then take the same scalp to the next rancher and collect an additional bounty. The ranchers soon caught on to the scam, and they stopped it by marking each scalp before returning it.

When caught in a trap, a lobo was not averse to chewing off the entrapped paw and limping away on the stump of a leg. Occasionally when following the trail of a lobo, the pursuer would be following tracks consisting of three paw prints plus the print of a stump. Those animals that had escaped from traps were much more difficult to trap a second time, and their endurance frequently inspired nicknames. Old Club Foot, Old Crip, Old Stubby, Old Two Toes, were typical names used. One such lobo, called Old Three Toes, eluded capture for so long and killed so many sheep, he attained a heroic status. When finally caught he was stuffed and displayed at the First National Bank at Memphis, Texas.

Daring, independent, proud, and crafty, the demise of the lobo symbolizes the demise of the frontier in the Southwest. The lobos possessed a nobility that is no longer to be seen.

Reference:

Winifred Kupper, *The Golden Hoof* (New York: Alfred A. Knopf, 1945).

The Lacey Dogs Brought in the Hogs

Llano County in Texas abounded in acorns and wild hogs. Because they lived in the wild, these hogs didn't know what an ear of corn looked like, but they relished the acorns that were free for the asking on the ground. Therefore, in years in which there was a bumper crop of acorns, there was also a bumper crop of fatted hogs to send to market. That is, if you could catch them.

Catching the hogs was one of the challenges the Lacey brothers took on after moving to Llano County from Tennessee. Riders on horseback can't corral the hogs because they run between the horses' legs, goring them with their tusks as they go. The riders can't rope them because they run with their noses close to the ground. Ordinary dogs can't handle the hogs either.

The Lacey brothers had three members of the canine family, none of which could be used for rounding up hogs. Frank Lacey had an English shepherd dog that was good at working sheep and cattle, but not hogs. John Lacey had a female greyhound, and George Lacey had a wolf that he kept tied to a live oak tree.

One day Frank got an idea. If they could merge the characteristics of these three animals into a three-way crossbreed, they might produce an animal having the natural herding instinct of the shepherd, the speed of the greyhound, and the stamina and trailing ability of the wolf. They succeeded in accomplishing the breeding, and the result was an instant success. The Laceys now were producing "hog" dogs that became known in those parts as Lacey dogs. Comparable in size to a wire-haired terrier, the Lacey dogs were reputed to be "tough as a boot, hard as nails, and enduring as a pocket knife."

A Lacey dog brought the hogs in by leading, not chasing them into the corrals. After finding a hog out in the open country, the Lacey dog would torment the hog and cause him to start squealing. Then, as a whole family of fifteen or twenty hogs rushed in to the rescue, the "Lacey" would circle about them at a safe distance and get them bunched together. Continuing to bark and snarl, the dog would tease the hogs until they got mad and started chasing him. Then off the Lacey would run, straight for the corral with the hogs hot on his tail. Inside the corral, the hogs would think they now had the dog cornered, but the dog merely jumped the corral fence as the men closed the gates of the corral. "The dog does it by instinct," Jake Winkel, a Llano County rancher claimed. "We don't teach him."

Lacey dogs were also useful for driving hogs to market. One local resident remembered his father buying several hundred hogs in Mason and driving them to the railroad pens at Llano. "Those hogs would string out like a bunch of steers. Out in front would be our old lead dog, Jep, with other dogs on the sides to keep them out of the brush."

Lacey dogs were prized animals. "I wouldn't take a thousand dollars for my dog if I couldn't get another," one rancher claimed. "My dog is worth the pay of ten men. Last year I gathered seventy head of fat hogs with my Lacey dog. So you see that dog was worth $3,000 to me in one season."

Reference:

Sam E. Harris, "Hog Dogs!," *True West*, January-February 1956.

Mules, Though Essential Beasts of Burden, Had Minds of Their Own

Despite all the jokes about mules and their stubbornness, those venerable beasts played essential roles in America's westward expansion. A New Mexico product, mules were introduced to Missourians in 1823 by Major Stephen Cooper, who traded a caravan of goods for four hundred mules at Santa Fe. They quickly became established fixtures in the freighting business. After proving their worth as beasts of burden, mules were used throughout Texas as well as in other areas for hauling goods and people. Many Texas settlers came from the East on the backs of dependable and inexpensive mules.

According to R. L. Duffus writing in *The Santa Fe Trail*, "Cooper's four-legged booty was apparently the beginning of the now world-renowned Missouri mule. He invaded Texas, Oklahoma, and Missouri from the west, filling a need which the rush of settlement into the river country was just beginning to create."

Along with oxen, mules proved to be invaluable beasts of burden, peculiarly suited to the rigorous and arid conditions of the Southwest. The mules were especially well adapted for traveling the arid expanses of the western portion of the Santa Fe Trail. According to Josiah Gregg in *Commerce of the Prairies*, "This animal is in fact to the Mexican what the camel has always been to the Arab—invaluable for the transportation of freight over sandy deserts and mountainous roads, where no other means of conveyance could be used to such advantage."

Mules can travel for hundreds of miles with bulky and unwieldy loads weighing three or four hundred pounds. There was no cheaper or more reliable transportation available.

The mules, however, were not the most cooperative of animals, and it frequently took a few hundred miles of traveling to work out their aversions to pulling wagons and carriages. It was a common occurrence for a mule to break away when being hitched, and some would run with chains and harness for a half hour or more until caught by men on horseback. Susan Shelby Magoffin, in her diary, tells of one mule that scampered off. After his pursuer finally succeeded in catching his bridle, the mule refused to turn or be led. "In defiance of all that man could do, he walked backwards all the way to camp leading his captor instead of being led."

Pack mules played a necessary role in taming the West

Photo courtesy of G. U. Hubbard Collection

The mules were truly useful animals, and they proved to be indispensable to the freighters. But they insisted on continuing to be mules.

Reference:

H. Gordon Frost, "The Santa Fe Trail," *Along the Early Trails of the Southwest* (Austin: The Pemberton Press, 1969).

An Army Experiment Backfires Literally

Because of the mobility of the Indians on the Great Plains, it was important to the U.S. Army to be equally mobile. Soldiers on horseback had this mobility, but when moving cannon through sand and through narrow mountain passes, the army had problems. Some way of making their artillery more mobile was needed. Many experiments were tried with very little success.

One novel experiment that was tried involved the use of mule-power. Because of the disastrous results, the names of the soldiers and the name of the fort were omitted from the account.

At one western fort an army major conceived the idea that artillery might be used more effectively against the Indians by strapping cannon to the backs of mules. After obtaining the permission of the fort's commanding officer, the major and a detachment of men brought a cannon and a mule to the edge of a stream adjacent to the fort. The men then strapped a howitzer to the back of the mule and loaded the weapon. Setting up a target in the middle of a stream, they brought the mule to the overlooking bluff and positioned the animal so that his back end and the muzzle of the cannon were pointing to the target. Standing around in a semicircle, the soldiers watched as the major lit the fuse of the cannon. Upon hearing the fizzing of the lighted fuse, the mule became uneasy, and then it went into a frenzy, whirling round and round. The soldiers scattered like flies and took cover wherever they could. When the cannon fired, the mule went over the bluff and the cannon ball went straight to the chimney of the major's quarters, frightening the major's wife into terrified convulsions as adobe bricks fell into the parlor.

The experiment was not tried again, and the War Department never received a report of the results.

Reference:

John Phoenix, *Encore*, Vol. VII, No. 38, April 1945.

The Elusive Southwest Mustangs Could Be Caught

In the 1500s Cortez, Pizarro, and other Spanish adventurers brought horses to the New World. Many of these horses strayed from their Spanish handlers, and unrestrained by humans or fences, they wandered and they multiplied. Three hundred years later, Anglo settlers moving into the Southwest encountered thousands of descendants of these earlier Spanish imports. These mustangs were free for the taking for anyone who could catch and tame them.

Although wild, the mustangs had definite behavior patterns. They banded together in small herds dominated by one of the stallions. Each herd had its territory, which it refused to leave or to which it always returned if forced out. Their grazing, drinking, and sleeping seemed to be on a regular daily schedule. Thus if a person studied a herd long enough, he could predict with reasonable accuracy where the herd would be or what route they would travel when moving on.

Catching one of these wild mustangs could be quite a challenge, and there were several ways of going about it. One

Mustang monument at University of Texas at Austin

Photo courtesy of G. U. Hubbard Collection

method was by using two men on foot. Although the method was sure, it could also be slow, sometimes requiring up to two weeks. Taking turns, two men on foot would follow a herd. At first they could get no closer than one half to three quarters of a mile, but after a few days the herd would become used to human presence. Then letting the human approach, the herd would ignore him and remain stationary until the human by his own actions started them in motion. With reasonable accuracy, the humans would know which direction the horses would go.

When ready to catch one of the horses, one person would conceal himself in a tree in the path the horses would be expected to travel, and the other person would set the herd in motion. As the herd passed under the tree, the person above would cast down his rope and snare one of the horses. This was a way for persons without horses to obtain them.

Another method, fast but not always certain, would be to "crease" the mustang. There is a very sensitive nerve on top of the horse's neck just in front of the shoulders. Creasing meant shooting a bullet into that nerve, the result of which would be to render the horse unconscious. After the person had time to tie and secure the horse, the animal would revive, the wound would heal, and the person would have a healthy horse in captivity. This was a risky method and sometimes fatal to the horse.

The mustangs, like the "wide, open spaces," were symbolic of unrestrained freedom. But man's perseverance and ingenuity tamed them as well as the land on which they flourished.

Reference:

Walter Prescott Webb, "Wild Horse Stories of Southwest Texas," *Round the Levee* (Dallas: Southern Methodist University Press, 1975).

"Jeff Davis's Folly" Was a Unique Experiment

An experiment in western American transportation, though conceded to have been a failure, is well worth remembering. Camels in America? Yes indeed! They were brought here to traverse the great American desert, but their survival was rather short lived.

Jefferson Davis, U.S. Senator from Mississippi, advocated the camels as early as 1853. A beast of burden that could navigate America's arid Southwest was needed, and that could only mean camels.

"We must have them," he drawled. "The men who are pushing through the desert and wilderness are shouting for an animal that can go without water for days and still carry a heavy pack on its back!"

When Davis later became secretary of war under President Franklin Pierce, he got his way by convincing Congress to appropriate $30,000 for the camel experiment. Men and ships were dispatched to the Middle East to purchase seventy-eight of the beasts and to hire some of their native keepers.

It appears that two shiploads of camels arrived in Texas in 1856; one in Indianola on Matagorda Bay and one at Parsons Pier in Galveston. Upon touching the ground in Indianola, some of the camels broke loose and stampeded in the area, frightening horses and people, before being brought under control by their keepers. In Galveston, after being hoisted from ship to shore in slings, about forty camels were herded into a nearby corral where they stayed for several months. Although a curiosity for the younger generation, the camels were unwelcome guests of the city. Whenever the keepers exercised the camels by riding them through the city streets, the horses and mules in the same streets frequently were terrorized and would stampede. In addition, the camels exuded a very offensive smell, and they would occasionally spit at people. But the young boys were delighted at getting to ride the camels at exercise time.

Finally the time came for the westward trek. The first major stop was at Camp Verde just north of San Antonio. Being keeper of the camels was a dubious honor for Colonel Robert E. Lee, Camp Verde's commander at the time. In an expedition from Camp Verde to the Big Bend of the Rio Grande, the U.S. Army proved that camels could outlast mules in adverse conditions or rugged terrain. Then in a caravan the camels were marched to California's Fort Tejon, just north of Los Angeles. But by the time they got to Fort Tejon, the Civil War had started, and interest in continuing the experiment waned. Their homesick keepers went home, and the soldiers didn't know how to handle the mangy beasts. So the government auctioned the camels to various buyers. Some went to circuses as curiosities. Some went to freight companies and construction companies as beasts of burden expected to be profitable, but they proved to be more trouble than they were worth. In 1864 Sam McLeneghan bought thirty-one of the beasts and placed them on his ranch in Sonoma County, California. On April 7, 1864, he promoted the "Great Camel Race" in Sacramento. River gamblers, Chinese laborers, and gaudy dance hall girls gathered to see the fun, but of the ten saddled camels that started the race, not one made it to the finish line. They were totally uncooperative. Nevertheless, the camels produced a unique excitement among the people wherever they went.

For several years people reported seeing stray camels wandering in various spots throughout the Southwest. Nevada even passed a law forbidding camels "from running at large on public highways." However, the law was rescinded in 1889 when it was realized that there weren't any wild camels left. The camels had had their day, but now it was over.

References:

Galveston Daily News, October 4, 1908.

Galveston Daily News, January 18, 1933.

Ethel Lindemood, "The Camels that Walked Miles for Uncle Sam," *Tempo Magazine*, October 31, 1968.

Old Rip Came to Life After a Long Sleep

After sleeping for thirty-one years, a West Texas horned toad startled everyone by coming back to life. As a result, the frog's admiring public in Eastland, Texas, gave him the name of Old Rip, a name inspired by Washington Irving's tale of Rip Van Winkle.

In 1897, as various mementos were being enshrined in the cornerstone of Eastland's new courthouse, Justice of the Peace Ernest Wood saw his son playing with a horned toad. "Why don't you put him in there also," Wood suggested, pointing to the cornerstone. The boy did just that, and the toad was sealed behind stone and mortar.

Thirty-one years later, when the courthouse building was being demolished to make way for a new building, a crowd of people gathered for the opening of the cornerstone. Old Rip was still there, and after a shake from Judge Ed Pritchard, a modern-day miracle was observed as the toad unexpectedly snapped back to life.

Becoming a celebrity, Old Rip toured the country, and he even visited President Calvin Coolidge at the White House. But

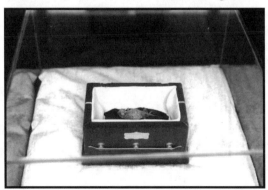

Old Rip on display at the Eastland County Courthouse

Photo courtesy of G. U. Hubbard Collection

old age overtook him, and he died within a year after his "resurrection." Stuffed by a taxidermist, Old Rip now rests in peace encased in glass in a plush velvet-lined box at Eastland's new courthouse.

Reference:

Ann Ruff, *Amazing Texas Monuments & Museums* (Houston: Lone Star Books, 1984).

The Dog That Was a Murder Witness

Shag (we'll call him that for want of his real name) didn't like the two men who came aboard his master's houseboat on October 14, 1895, when it was docked on the Red River near Arthur City, just north of Paris, Texas. Shag's master, a man named Kennedy, had to restrain the animal as he growled at the two men who had come aboard to have a harness repaired.

Kennedy earned his living by cruising up and down the Red River between Texas and Indian Territory and repairing almost anything brought to him. Making repairs by day, he spent most evenings playing poker with friends who would come aboard at each stopping place. Kennedy earned a good living at his trade, and it was generally believed that he kept a large sum of money on board.

As the two men with the harness left the boat, three friends came aboard to spend the night with Kennedy. Hiding in the nearby bushes, the two men waited until the lights on the boat were extinguished, and then they came back on board with the intent of robbing Kennedy and his friends. Although it is not clear how the tragedy unfolded, the end result was that Kennedy and his three friends were all murdered. Shag, in trying to protect his master, received a severe cut on the head and was left for dead.

The next morning a farmer out rounding up his cattle noticed that the boat had not left its mooring, so he went aboard to see if anything was wrong. After discovering the four dead bodies, the farmer raced into Paris to report the crime, and Marshal Shep Williams and a deputy came out to investigate. It took a lot of coaxing to get Shag, who had revived, to allow them to come on board.

Marshal Williams assigned Jim Chancellor to the case, and after several weeks of questioning residents on both sides of the river, Chancellor identified Silas Lee and Willis Hickman as the two culprits. They were immediately arrested and brought to trial at Paris.

The testimonies and evidence given during the trial were mostly circumstantial until the prosecution brought in a surprise witness—Shag. Shag immediately recognized Lee and Hickman, and although on a leash, he sprang toward them growling and with teeth bared to sink into their throats. It was all the handler could do to restrain the furious dog. There was no longer any doubt in anyone's mind regarding the guilt of Lee and Hickman. The judge was convinced, and one of the jurors later said, "had no other testimony been given than that of the dog, it would have been enough."

As the trial ended, Shag was allowed also to examine some of the clothing of the four victims that had been brought into the courtroom. Sniffing at each bundle, he stopped when he got to Kennedy's bundle, and he quietly lay down beside it as if to guard it.

Jim Chancellor kept Shag for a short time after the trial and then sent the animal to Princeton, Indiana, to live with members of the Kennedy family at their request.

Reference:

Louise Riotte, "The Dog Who Was a Murder Witness," *Frontier Times*, October-November 1975.

Neighbors

Introduction

J ust as we acknowledge that "no man is an island," we should also acknowledge that no state is an island. Bordered on three sides by New Mexico, Oklahoma, Arkansas, and Louisiana, the state of Texas has received much and given much to its neighbors.

The influence of early Spanish occupation was clearly evident in Texas and New Mexico, and these two entities shared similar border problems with Mexico. Indians constituted another element of commonality, especially with the Comanches primarily in Texas and what is now Oklahoma, and the Apaches primarily in Texas and New Mexico. Gunslingers operated rather freely in all three areas.

During the years of the Confederacy and the Civil War, Texas had much in common with Arkansas and Louisiana and the rest of the South. Louisiana also served as a land of refuge for the Runaway Scrape, the exodus of Texians fleeing the advancing Mexican armies during Texas's fight for independence.

The influences worked in both directions, with Texas contributing to and receiving from its neighbors. A selection of vignettes from Texas's neighbors seems appropriate in this volume. Each of these stories shows a relationship with Texas.

Two Friends Save Each Other's Lives

Things were tense along the Texas and New Mexico borders during Pancho Villa's forays in northern Mexico. In 1916 citizens of El Paso were especially fearful that Villa would cross the Rio Grande at Juarez and attempt to ravage their city.

Villa, who had planned to subdue the Mexican state of Sonora, was furious that the United States had allowed armed Mexican nationals to enter Texas at Eagle Pass and then travel by train over United States soil through El Paso and on to Arizona to reinforce the Sonoran defenders below the border. After being mauled and defeated at Auga Prieta in Sonora, Villa decided to give vent to his rage by raiding Columbus, New Mexico, as a token of retaliation against the United States.

"We're going to kill gringos, boys," he told his decimated troops on the eve of the attack.

With loud shouting and shooting, Villa's forces galloped into Columbus early on the morning of March 9, 1916, awakening the peacefully sleeping citizens. Guests at the Commercial Hotel fled in panic as did the local citizenry. At least ten Americans were killed as the Mexicans thoroughly sacked and then burned the hotel, the grocery stores, and several other buildings.

Chaos and pandemonium reigned everywhere. The enigma of the situation is that Colonel Herbert J. Slocum, who

Ruins of Columbus, NM after raid by Pancho Villa

Photo courtesy of Texas State Library and Archives Commission

commanded a U.S. Army detachment at Columbus, had been warned the night before that an attack was coming, but Slocum chose to ignore the warning.

At the time of the attack, Laura Ritchie, wife of the hotel's manager, was asleep with her three daughters in their hotel apartment. It's nice to have a friend when you need one, and on this occasion, Laura was very glad to have one. Laura had been friendly with a Yaqui Indian named Juan Favela, who was employed as a servant of the Ritchies. Considering Favela as more of a family member than a servant, she always made sure that he had plenty to eat, and she did other niceties for him whenever she could. A strong bond of friendship and loyalty existed between the two.

When the attack started, Favela proved to be a friend indeed. Dashing into the hotel through the back door, Favela broke down Mrs. Ritchie's door and managed to convince her and her daughters of what was happening outside. He led the four half-dressed women outside and concealed them where they would be safe, shooting two Villistas in the process. Unfortunately, Favela was unable to save Mr. Ritchie, who was killed in the attack.

An interesting postscript is that after the attack, American authorities arrested Favela and were going to hang him for complicity with the Mexicans. It was this same Favela who knew in advance of the coming attack and who had tried to warn the Americans. Opportune testimony by Mrs. Ritchie and her daughters saved his life.

They say that true friendship knows no bounds. In this case, each friend survived the ordeal because of the helpful intervention of the other.

References:

Elias L. Torres, *Twenty Episodes in the Life of Pancho Villa* (Austin: The Encino Press, 1973).

Joseph Raymond Monticone, "Revolutionary Mexico and the U.S. Southwest: The Columbus Raid" (Master of Arts Thesis at California State University, Fullerton, 1981).

The Americans Prevail at the Battle of Brazito

It was going to be a gloomy Christmas for Colonel Alexander Doniphan's First Missouri Mounted Volunteers. As participants in the Mexican-American War, their job was to occupy Paseo del Norte (now known as El Paso) and hold it as a staging point for military excursions into the Mexican province of Chihuahua. Marching through southeastern New Mexico on Christmas morning of 1845, the Missourians were a dispirited and loosely organized group.

While good as fighting men, the volunteers were quite lax on military discipline. They were really a fun-loving group of civilians. Many wore fringed hunting shirts and pantaloons. Most of their faces were so bearded it seemed as though they were looking through bearskins. But they were fighters, and they loved their commander who was "not afraid of the Devil or the God that made him."

After marching eighteen miles that Christmas morning, the Missourians began arriving at the Brazito, a tributary of the Rio Grande between Las Cruces and El Paso. Doniphan ordered a halt, and they began making camp. Although their wagons were strung out for miles, the Missourians' close proximity to Paseo del Norte stirred the Mexicans to necessary action. When sentries noticed clouds of dust rising on the southern horizon, Doniphan sent scouts out to investigate. Returning to the camp, the scouts reported that Lt. Col. Ponce de Leon and a force of Mexicans were advancing on the Missourians' camp. Doniphan at the time was enjoying a card game with a captured Mexican horse as the prize. Throwing down his cards, Doniphan proclaimed, "We must stop this game long enough to whip the Mexicans, but remember that I am way ahead in the score and cannot be beaten, and we will play it out as soon as the battle is over." With that, the bugle blew and the scattered Missourians scurried to their guns and horses.

As the Mexicans approached, they sent an emissary to seek a peaceful settlement. Carrying a black flag with double skulls and crossbones on one side and the words "Libertad O Muerto" on the other side, the emissary asked that the American commander come and meet with Ponce de Leon. Rejecting this request, the American emissary, Thomas Caldwell, suggested if the Mexicans really wanted to avoid hostilities, then Ponce de Leon should come to the American camp to meet with Col. Doniphan. Although the negotiating proved fruitless, it gave the Missourians time to group themselves into battle formation.

As the Mexican force galloped forward, Doniphan ordered his men to hold their fire until the Mexicans were within 100 yards. When the firing commenced, the Mexicans were badly beaten, and within thirty minutes the battle was over and the Mexicans were routed.

The Missourians spent the next day burying the soldiers on both sides who had been killed. Then on December 27 they completed their mission by entering and occupying Paseo del Norte. The first battle of the Mexican-American War to be fought on New Mexico soil ended in a great victory for the Americans who went on and occupied El Paso as ordered.

Reference:

Neil C. Mangum, "The Battle of Brazito: Reappraising a Lost and Forgotten Episode in the Mexican-American War," *New Mexico Historical Review*, July 1997.

Bill Chunk Tries to Get the Best of Clay Allison

Clay Allison was called "a whale of a fellow with a gun." Those who knew him didn't cross him. Born in Tennessee about 1840, Allison fought on the Confederate side in the Civil War and afterward maintained his hatred for the northerners. Following the war he drifted around in Indian Territory, Texas and New Mexico, where he won fame as a deadly gunslinger.

Allison was strongly built at 6 feet 2 inches and about 190 pounds. He was active and quick despite a slight limp caused by shooting himself in the foot a few years earlier. When sober he was a perfect gentleman, but when drunk, it was best to stay away from him. Drunk or sober, he never backed away from a challenge.

After a few drinks, Allison's wild, reckless conduct showed itself in a variety of ways. There was the time when he appeared stark naked except for his sombrero, boots, and pistol belt and rode his horse the length of Main Street in Canadian, Texas, shouting unprintable taunts to the horrified women as he passed. Dismounting at a saloon, he invited the curious spectators inside for drinks.

On another occasion Allison was spending time at a hostelry called the Clifton House near the site of present-day Raton, New Mexico. Bill Chunk was also there. Being somewhat jealous of Allison's fame and the high regard others had for Allison's abilities with a gun, Chunk, who claimed to have killed fourteen men himself, boasted that Allison would be number fifteen. Allison had no intention of backing off or of letting that happen.

For a day and a night, Chunk and Allison drank and caroused together, outwardly appearing to be friends. Not finding the opening he sought, Chunk proposed the next day that they have a horse race to see who had the better animal.

Chunk won the race. As a result, Allison lost his temper and slapped Chunk in the face, but hostilities still didn't begin. Wanting to regain his honor, Allison then suggested that they duel it out on horseback. He proposed that they mount their horses one hundred yards apart and gallop toward each other, firing their guns until one of them dropped. Chunk voiced his willingness, but then the dinner bell sounded. "We ought to see that the dead one goes to hell with a full stomach," he suggested.

Clay Allison was an outlaw of daring exploits

Photo courtesy of Western History Collections, University of Oklahoma Libraries

In the dining hall the two men sat at opposite ends of the table facing each other. Both had their six-shooters on their laps under the table. During the meal, Chunk dropped his hand casually then jerked up his gun, but the barrel hit the edge of the table and his shot went awry. Just as quickly, Allison had his gun up and fired one shot, hitting Chunk just above the eye. Chunk slumped forward dead, and his face fell into the plate of food he had been eating.

"Everyone stay where you are and continue eating," Allison ordered. Replacing his pistol in its holster, he leisurely finished his meal, then went outside and, calling everyone together, he announced, "Gentlemen, the proposed fight is now off, owing to an accident to one of the principals."

References:

Maurice G. Fulton, "Clay Allison," *Southwest Review*, Winter 1930.

Norman B. Wiltsey, "Laughing Killer," *True West*, August 1956.

When the Frisco Crossed the Katy

The railroad builders tied this land together with the cunning, courage, ingenuity, and humor that equals anything we have come to expect of the trappers, traders, miners, and homesteaders. When it came to being "men to match my mountains," the railroaders didn't take a back seat to anyone. They not only competed with and beat the terrain and the elements, they also competed with each other for the lucrative markets. And therein lie some of the best of tales.

Take the race into Indian Territory and on to Texas between the Missouri-Kansas-Texas Railroad (known as the Katy) and the St. Louis-San Francisco Railroad (known as the Frisco). As the first railroad into Indian Territory, the Katy established the town of Downingville (now Vinita, Oklahoma) to be a gateway for wagon trains to the Southwest. Learning that the Frisco also had government permission to build through the current location of Downingville, the Katy sought to avoid sharing the town by relocating it two miles south. But the good citizens of Downingville didn't take kindly to such a move, so Downingville stayed where it was with the Frisco knocking at the door.

Determined to retain its first-rights to the Indian Territory in one way or another, the Katy determined another scheme to impede the Frisco's progress. If Downingville couldn't be moved, neither would the Katy allow the Frisco to cross its tracks even though, by law, they could not prevent it. Even a few days delay would benefit the Katy's cause.

As the showdown approached, the work crews of both lines began to swell with additional manpower, many of whom seemed more adept at handling guns than shovels. The Frisco built up to the proposed point of intersection, but there they were stymied. A Katy work train had the crossing point blocked, and it intended to stay there. The law required the train to keep moving, but it didn't have to move very far. So it kept reversing directions and kept the crossing point sufficiently blocked to thwart the Frisco. This went on for two days while the Frisco brass fumed. But they weren't without their own bag of tricks, and on the third day they were ready.

When the Katy train stopped to reverse directions, a long line of prairie schooners moved in behind the train and started crossing the tracks, slowly and leisurely, in single file. By the time the last wagon had crossed, the first wagon had circled around and was right behind it. The schooners had the Katy train encircled and trapped because wagon trains had priority. When the train was "released" a few hours later, the engineer raced back to the crossing point, but he was too late. The Frisco had crossed the Katy.

As the railroads built westward and southward, rivalry and subterfuge were a natural part of the competitive environment. Although the Frisco won this confrontation, the Katy had its share of other victories and eventually was the first railroad into Texas from the north.

Reference:

Vincent Victor Masterson, *The Katy Railroad and the Last Frontier* (Norman: University of Oklahoma Press, 1952).

Jim (Killer) Miller Pulls One Job Too Many

On April 19, 1909, four men were lynched by a mob of citizens in Ada, Oklahoma, in reprisal for the murder of A. A. (Gus) Bobbitt, a wealthy Ada cattleman. One of the hanged men was James B. (Killer) Miller, a Texan reputed to have killed more than twenty persons during his lifetime.

The enigma about Jim Miller is that he appeared to be such a peaceful and pious citizen. He neither smoked, drank, gambled, nor cursed. He dressed well and attended church regularly. A man of excellent manners, he was especially courteous to the ladies. This righteous and courteous exterior was a valuable asset, for wherever he lived he became respected and well liked by all who knew him in a purely social capacity.

Miller's outward demeanor had a winning charm that served him well in a number of instances. On one occasion Miller was scheduled to be tried in Eastland, Texas, for the murder of Bud Frazer. Moving to Eastland well in advance of the trial, he became a hotel operator there. He transferred his church membership, attended services faithfully, and cultivated the friendship of Eastland's most prominent citizens. When his case came to court, he was well supplied with character witnesses who came forward to attest to his good citizenship. The trial ended with a hung jury, and on retrial Miller was acquitted.

Jim Miller was a well-known professional gunman who seemed to delight in shedding blood. It is said that he would kill any man for a price. Dee Harkey, a law enforcement officer who once arrested Miller and who had numerous encounters with him, called him "the meanest outlaw in West Texas or New Mexico." Miller is reported to have killed over twenty white men in his lifetime plus an uncounted number of "Mexicans along the border." He was arrested and tried on numerous occasions but had always managed to escape punishment.

Born in Van Buren, Arkansas, Miller spent most of his life in West Texas. He earned his legitimate livelihood as a hotel operator in Pecos, Eastland, Memphis, and Fort Worth. He also served for short periods as a Texas Ranger and as a deputy sheriff. One report says he once served as a deputy U.S. marshal. Just as Dr. Jekyll had an alter ego, so did Jim Miller.

Gus Bobbitt, one of Ada, Oklahoma's most respected and influential citizens, was the unfortunate object of Miller's last "job." Bobbitt lived on a ranch seven miles southwest of Ada where he had engaged in a very successful cattle business. Besides being a cattleman, he was also a former law enforcement officer, having served many years as a deputy U.S. marshal and later as Ada city marshal. In these capacities he had earned the reputation of being a fearless defender of justice. He had sent many lawbreakers to jail and had incurred the wrath and sworn vengeance of some of them. Although Bobbitt was no longer serving in a law enforcement capacity, he had made provision in his will of $1,000 for the prosecution of his killers should such a thing occur.

It is believed that two of Bobbitt's sworn enemies, Joe Allen and Jesse West, hired Miller to do the job for $2,000. B. B. Burrell served as Miller's spotter. Moving from Fort Worth to Ada, Miller spent several weeks as a "citizen" until sensing the right opportunity. On Saturday, February 27, 1909, Burrell saw Bobbitt in Ada loading his wagon with cottonseed meal. Burrell rode out to Miller's house to tell him that Bobbitt would be driving past soon, and he described the team of horses pulling Bobbitt's wagon. Miller mounted a yellow horse he kept at the house, rode down the road to a place of concealment about a mile from Bobbitt's ranch, and waited. As Bobbitt rode by that evening, Miller shot him in the back from ambush.

When news of the shooting became public, the citizens of Ada were wild with fury, and the four perpetrators were quickly apprehended. Miller, who had returned to Texas, was arrested in a house on Dozier Creek about fourteen miles northwest of Fort Worth. The suspects were placed in custody in the jail at Ada where they awaited a preliminary hearing that began on

April 16. After hearing the prosecution recount the crime, Ada's citizens were again stirred to a fever pitch. There was no doubt in anyone's mind that these were the guilty men. And after hearing a recount of Miller's previous exploits, which had all gone unpunished, they literally went wild.

Late in the evening a crowd of people began to gather downtown, and mob action was at hand. County Judge Joel Terrell and County Attorney Robert Wimbish learned of the mob's plans and pleaded with its leaders to abandon their intentions, but to no avail. The two men were advised to go home and not interfere. Later Terrell was on the street again, and with night policeman Lee West he tried again to disperse the mob, but threats on his own life caused him to retire a second time.

The mob continued to gather and grow until 2:00 A.M. when they went into action. Two of their number went to the city power plant, and with pistols in hand, they "ordered" the streetlights shut off for an hour. The mob then entered the courthouse and made their way to the jail in the rear of the building.

Pounding on the door of the jail, one of the mob's leaders demanded entrance, shouting, "Sheriff, we mean business."

"You might as well go home, boys," came the reply from inside. "I will never open this door. Duty is duty. I'm here to observe the law and protect these men."

Without further conversation, four of the mob fell against the door, breaking it open. Once inside, the mob quickly overpowered and bound the two night guards. Moving to the next

The lynching at Ada, Oklahoma

Photo courtesy of Western History Collections, University of Oklahoma Libraries

room where deputy sheriffs Walter Goyne and Robert Nestor had been staying, they took the keys to the cells from Goyne. When Nestor tried to resist, one of the mob clubbed him with a revolver and tied him hand and foot. Failing to get the cell doors unlocked, they forced Goyne into the cell corridor and made him open the heavy doors. They then bound him also.

Miller was taken from his cell first, and his hands were tied with bailing wire. West fought like a demon until he was struck on the head with a revolver, a blow that fractured his skull. The other two suspects came peacefully.

The mob carried their four captives to an abandoned livery stable only forty feet away, and there they carried out their intentions. Each of their prisoners was placed on a white horse and strung to the crossbeams of the barn, the horse then being driven out from under his "load." It was all done quickly and quietly, nothing official being known of it until daylight. When the four bodies were discovered, the white horse was still in the barn. The bodies were cut down and taken to the local funeral home to await claim by relatives.

Miller remained calm through the entire ordeal. It is reported that his only words were, "You men have a job to do. Go ahead with it."

Reference:

George U. Hubbard, "The Lynching of 'Killer' Miller," *True Frontier,* March 1969.

The Last Man to Die by Creek Law

On January 1, 1896, Timmie Jack, a Creek Indian, killed his friend James Brown in a drunken brawl at an Indian dance on the Creek reservation in Oklahoma. At Timmie Jack's trial, held on April 28, he was found guilty and sentenced to die on May 1. Creek law required execution for such a crime, and by Creek custom, death by shooting was the only acceptable method. White men might be pardoned or paroled for murder, but not so within the Indians' own laws.

The unique aspect of this episode is that Timmie Jack was never arrested or held in jail. He was simply told to be on hand for the trial at the Creek District Court House in Okmulgee. On the appointed day he was there. After the guilty verdict and the sentencing, he was told to go home and settle his affairs but to be at the Council House on May 1 prepared to pay his penalty. Again, he was there.

The day of execution was almost a gala occasion. Indians gathered from miles around with their families. White settlers and cowboys came. Picnic lunches were eaten under the shady elm trees. Timmie Jack mingled among the throng all day, introduced himself to those he did not know, and exchanged pleasantries with all. He could not say goodbye because there is no such word in the Creek language. But he did use a phrase that means "I will see you again, some where, some time."

Creek custom allowed Timmie Jack to name the time of execution and to name the executioner. Timmie chose Pleasant Berryhill, a captain in the Creek tribal police and one of the best shots in the Creek nation. Timmie wanted it to be as quick and painless as possible. Five o'clock was the designated hour.

Berryhill asked to borrow a rifle, because his own was in a scabbard on his horse over a block away. But Timmie said no. "Get your own Winchester. You know how it shoots." Timmie then embraced his family and friends for the last time, seated himself on a box, and leaned back against one of the elms. No

279

blindfold or bands were offered, nor would they have been accepted. A white doctor used his stethoscope to locate the exact position of Timmie's heart, and pinned a piece of white paper on the spot. Berryhill, 15 feet away, braced his Winchester on an elm tree, and for almost a full minute he and Timmie looked at each other eye to eye. Then Berryhill's rifle cracked, Timmie slumped forward, and the execution was completed. Because the Creek nation was submitting itself to the laws of the recently formed Territory of Oklahoma, this was the last execution under Creek law.

Reference:

Museum of the Five Civilized Tribes at Muskogee, Oklahoma.

Moses and Stephen F. Austin Participated in Founding Little Rock, Arkansas

When the Territory of Arkansas was organized in 1819, no designation of a permanent capital city was made. The issue would be decided by the territorial legislature when it met the following year. Cadron and Little Rock became the two major contenders for the coveted designation. Although Little Rock was nothing more than a prominent rock formation and a ferry across the Arkansas River, it lay where the "Missouri Road" (from Missouri to Texas) crossed the Arkansas River and therefore appeared to be a very favorable location.

During this same period of time, Moses Austin, with visions of wealth and grandeur, was making arrangements and collecting applications for the colony he planned to establish in Texas.

Stephen F. Austin
Photo courtesy of Center for American History, The University of Texas

Having obtained a large grant of land in Texas, Moses persuaded his son, Stephen F., and his son-in-law, James Bryan, to join him in his grand colonizing venture. As a group they established the community of Fulton in southern Arkansas on the Red River where they hoped to make money replenishing the food and supplies of the anticipated migrations who would be coming from Missouri and the northeast. They were smart enough to recognize that if they also established a town at Little Rock and if it became the capital of Arkansas, they would become even wealthier. In addition, Little Rock would be another natural spot for rest and replenishing of supplies of Texas-bound immigrants traveling the Missouri Road.

Stephen F. Austin campaigned to become Arkansas' delegate to Congress, and although he lost by a narrow margin, he nevertheless established helpful contacts among the Arkansas politicos. William O'Hara, who had been a cashier in a bank owned by Moses Austin in St. Louis, joined the Austins in their ventures. Through his banking connections and his own expertise in real estate speculation, O'Hara managed to come into possession of three unused "New Madrid Certificates." These certificates, issued by the federal government to citizens of New Madrid, Missouri, following a disastrous earthquake in their area, entitled the bearer the right to resettle, free of charge, on any unclaimed land within the United States. With these certificates, the Austin group made claim to land at Little Rock and proceeded to lay out a town.

In the meantime, Stephen F. Austin had been appointed judge of Arkansas' First Judicial Circuit, replacing the man who beat him in the congressional election. In this position, Austin campaigned vigorously for the capital to be located at Little Rock. Of even greater influence was the pressure brought by William Russell, sometimes known as the "Father of Arkansas." In competition with the Austins, Russell also claimed Little Rock, but their efforts were united in seeking the capital. Although the legislature vacillated considerably on the issue, Little Rock became the permanent capital in June 1821.

For many years the controversies of land ownership in Little Rock raged. Moses Austin died in 1821, and with Stephen and his brother-in-law thoroughly immersed in the colonization of Texas, William Russell gradually assumed the dominant role in the matter. The Austins dropped out of the picture, leaving Russell to fight off other contenders who tried to move in on the lucrative opportunities offered by the new capital of Arkansas.

Reference:

Dallas T. Herndon, *Why Little Rock Was Born* (Little Rock: Central Printing Company, 1933).

Judge Parker Was Known as the Hanging Judge

In 1875 Isaac C. Parker became a federal judge in Fort Smith, then considered by many to be the toughest town in the United States. In administering justice to an area ranging from the Colorado border in the west to the Arkansas River to the east, Judge Parker converted what had been an almost completely lawless area into an area where punishment for wrongdoing was swift, severe, and certain. In so doing, he brought a semblance of peace, safety, and orderliness to an area that had been without.

Where capital offenses were involved, hanging was the judge's usual form of sentencing. The record indicates that during his tenure, he sentenced 172 people to be hanged, thus earning for himself the title of "the hanging judge." For a variety of reasons, only 88 were actually hanged. Some prisoners escaped, some died in prison, some received new trials from appeals, and some were commuted to life imprisonment by the president of the United States.

Judge Isaac C. Parker
Photo courtesy of
Western History Collections,
University of Oklahoma Libraries

Probably the worst gang of outlaws to appear before Judge Parker was the Rufus Buck gang, who were convicted of many instances of murder, rape, and other heinous crimes. They were all hanged quickly. On the other hand, the infamous Belle Starr appeared five times before Parker, but not for capital crimes.

One of the frustrations of Parker's career was his attempts to hang a man named Frank Carver.

283

Having spent most of his life in Texas and in the unorganized Indian country, Carver came to Fort Smith where he met Annie Maledon, a beautiful local girl who was still unattached. Showered with attentions that she had never received from the local boys, Annie became blindly attracted to Carver. Gradually she learned that Carver was a whiskey runner in Texas and a gambler. What was worse, Carver was an "allotment gambler," which meant that whenever the Indians got their allotment money from the federal government, he would cheat them out of it. For long periods of time, Carver would disappear into Texas on drinking and gambling sprees and to bring liquor back to Arkansas. Despite all this, Annie Maledon was Carver's "girl." Even the revelation that Carver already had an Indian wife and two children in Muskogee did not dissuade her.

Then on a trip to Muskogee, Carver became convinced that Annie was cheating on him, and in a jealous rage, he shot her. Severely wounded but still alive, Annie was rushed back to Fort Smith where she died eleven weeks later in the hospital.

Judge Parker, who had known Annie all her life, was deeply moved by the tragedy. Although he usually did not show his emotions in court cases, this time the judge remarked to a deputy that he looked forward to hanging Carver. But the hanging never occurred. Three times Carver was tried. The first two times he was convicted and sentenced by Parker to be hanged. But each time, Carver's attorney managed to get the ruling reversed through technicalities. In the third trial the attorney brought in new witnesses who swore that Carver was somewhere else at the time of the shooting, and the confused jury brought in a sentence of life imprisonment.

Despite occasional reverses such as the Carver case, Judge Parker succeeded in instituting law and order when it had previously been absent.

Reference:

Homer Croy, *He Hanged Them High* (New York: Duell, Sloan, and Pearce, 1952).

De Queen Was Peaceful While "Old Dike" Was Marshal

Marshal Dycus, known affectionately as "Old Dike," was a law and order man who was not afraid of those who sometimes challenged him. Efficient as well as fearless, even with a wooden leg, Dycus maintained a peaceful environment in the late 1800s as marshal in De Queen, in the southwest corner of Arkansas. Because De Queen, formerly known as Hurrah City, was located where the Fort Towson Trail crossed a well-traveled route into Texas, maintaining a peaceful environment was quite an accomplishment. The town's close proximity to the Indian Territory made matters even more challenging.

In maintaining law and order, Old Dike's most persistent problem was in dealing with the stray dogs that John Wright kept adopting at the De Horse Hotel that his mother operated. On the other hand, the peg-legged Dycus was never known to avoid a fight or to refuse to go wherever needed. He also had a sense of humor that seemed to emerge under trying situations.

One time when a drunk appeared at the scene of a barbecue and celebration on the courthouse lawn, Dycus accosted the drunk and told him he was under arrest. Being quite a bit larger than the marshal, the drunk resisted the arrest, and it became evident that Dycus would have to fight him all the way to the jail. Sensing that Dycus could use some help, two men came forward offering their assistance.

"Thank you kindly, gents," Dycus said. "If I don't have him locked up by supper time, then you can come and fight him while I eat."

On another occasion, while he was trying to arrest a man who was younger and more agile, a fight between the two ensued, and Dycus found himself on the ground. In those days if one assailant should try to stomp an opponent who was on the ground, the crowd would intervene and deal with the unfair fighter. But in this case the younger man, trying to break Dycus's leg by stomping on it, stomped the wooden peg, fell, and shook himself up. The crowd didn't need to intervene. Instead they laughed the assailant out of town.

Old Dike's first name is not known, nor is it remembered how long he served as marshal. But De Queen, with a population exceeding 2,000 in 1899, owes a debt of gratitude to its marshal who maintained the peace despite the prevailing lawlessness in that general area of the Southwest.

Reference:

Harold Mabry, "Hotel De Horse," *True West*, July-August 1979.

Billy Bowlegs Captivates New Orleans

Billy Bowlegs, whose Indian name was Halpatter-Micco, was the last chief of the Florida Seminoles. He was also a warrior, and as such he gave the U.S. Army fits. Of all the Indian tribes in the Southeast, the Seminoles were the most resistant to Andrew Jackson's policy of removing them to Indian Territory in present-day Oklahoma. Against federal troops the Seminoles fought and won three wars, one of which lasted seven years. Although pushed back into the swampy Everglades, Bowlegs and his forces thwarted every attempt to dislodge them. Bowlegs beat Colonel William S. Harney. He also beat General Zachary Taylor.

Following the First Seminole War (1812-1814), the Second Seminole War began in 1835 and lasted until 1842 when the federal government tired of pursuing it any further. It has been reported that President John Tyler commented at the time, "The further pursuit of these miserable beings by a large military force seems to be as injudicious as it is unavailing."

Finally, after the third war, the aging Bowlegs accepted a government offer of $6,500 plus $100 for each of his four subchiefs, plus $500 for each warrior plus $100 for each woman and child. Being weary from so much fighting, Billy

Chief Billy Bowlegs created quite a stir in New Orleans

Photo courtesy of
Western History Collections,
University of Oklahoma Libraries

and all but about 300 Seminoles accepted the inducement to move from Florida to Indian Territory. (The 300 remained in the swamps, and their descendants are in Florida to this day.) Setting out for their new home, Bowlegs and his followers made a brief, but memorable, stop in New Orleans.

Arriving in New Orleans in May 1858, Billy Bowlegs led a company that included two wives, one son, five daughters, fifty slaves, and $100,000 in cold hard cash. A *Harper's Weekly* correspondent described the fifty-year-old Billy as "about 160 pounds, fine forehead, keen black eyes, and somewhat above medium height." Billy proudly wore two medals around his neck, one of President Martin Van Buren and one of President Millard Fillmore.

King Billy and his entourage were quite a spectacle in New Orleans, and although he spent most of his time in an intoxicated state, the city treated him royally. Accepting an invitation to visit the local museum, Bowlegs toured its rooms accompanied by three faithful braves who kept him cool by fanning him, and he thirstily drank the punch provided. This Seminole chief, who boasted that he had killed a hundred white men in one day, thanked his white brothers for their "much friendship" and swore he would never leave them as long as they gave him "as much punch" as he wanted. Bowlegs was especially attracted to the wax figures of prominent U.S. Army officers. "Scott and Taylor," he said, "were great men and fought me mighty hard." But of Harney, Bowlegs said he made him "run like hell."

Bowlegs also submitted to a three-hour photography session at Clark's Photographic Gallery. A hand-colored version of one of Clark's pictures is currently hanging as a portrait in the Seminole Nation Museum in Wewoka, Oklahoma, and is available as a picture postcard in the local museum in Fort Meyers, Florida.

While in New Orleans, Bowlegs took such a liking to the *Harper's* correspondent that he offered him his daughter as a wife. "Betsy—good squaw—never married—you have her—come with me—I make you great chief—next after me." The correspondent graciously declined, but it turned out that Betsy was also available to any other white man who would pay a dowry of $10,000 in hard cash.

From New Orleans, Bowlegs and his company traveled by boat to Fort Gibson, Oklahoma, where they settled with other Seminoles who had migrated earlier. Bowlegs' story becomes cloudy at this point, and there are conflicting accounts of his remaining activities. When the American Civil War broke out in 1861, the Seminoles and the Creeks sided with the Union, and disputed accounts say that Billy Bowlegs and over a hundred of his warriors joined with Union forces, and that Bowlegs was commissioned a captain.

It is clear, however, that Bowlegs' heritage lives on in place names in Oklahoma as well as in Florida. In Oklahoma, there is a Bowlegs Oil Field, and a town named Bowlegs located in Seminole County. A tombstone bearing the name of Billy Bowlegs stands in the Officers' Circle of the National Cemetery at Fort Gibson, although there is doubt by some that the great Seminole warrior and chief is actually buried there.

An undisputed honor is that a portrait of Chief Billy Bowlegs, this Seminole warrior who had earlier fought so bitterly and successfully against federal forces in Florida, hangs in the Smithsonian Institute in Washington, D.C. And he is proudly remembered to this day by numerous posterity in both Florida and Oklahoma.

References:

George U. Hubbard, "Billy Bowlegs: The Seminole Chief Who Wouldn't Be Subdued," *Old West*, Winter 1998.

John K. Mahon, *History of the Second Seminole War* (Gainesville: University of Florida Press, 1967).

The Civil War Also Had Its Humane Side

Having been repulsed at Sabine Pass by Lieutenant Dick Dowling and a relative handful of Irishmen from Houston, the remnants of a Union armada carrying an invading Northern army landed safely on Louisiana soil. Here they hoped things would go better than their attempted invasion of Texas.

As the invading force proceeded northward toward Opelousas, a Confederate force encountered and captured a number of stragglers from the Union army. The Confederate general immediately wrote a letter to General William R. Miles, commander of the Louisiana district, announcing the capture and stating that the prisoners would be sent to headquarters the next day. Unfortunately the letter fell into Union hands when the Yankees captured the courier bearing the letter, and it was delivered instead to General Wickham Hoffman, adjutant with the invading force.

Although history is filled with seeming coincidences, it is nevertheless interesting that General Hoffman was personally acquainted, from earlier years in New Orleans, with the letter writer and with the letter writer's charming Creole wife. Here was an opportunity to perform a humane service. Sending the letter to the wife, Hoffman added his own note to the effect that she had probably not seen her husband's handwriting for some time and she might be gratified to learn from the enclosed letter that her husband was well. "I shall spare no pains to capture the general himself and send him to you; and if he knew what fate was in store for him, I am sure he would make but a feeble resistance."

The grateful wife replied that with such generous enemies, the war lost half its terrors. Although the Union army recaptured its lost prisoners, the fate of the letter-writing Confederate general is not known.

The humanitarian General Hoffman had additional opportunities to correspond with southerners. One other instance will be cited.

At New Orleans, the Union soldiers seized a bag of Rebel correspondence as it was about to cross Lake Pontchartrain. In one of the letters, a lady named Anna bragged to her brother-in-law in Mobile of a trick she had successfully played on a Boston newspaper. Anna had sent a poem, "The Gypsy's Wassail," to the newspaper along with the claim that she had translated it from Sanscrit. She had also sent the following as an example of the Sanscrit.

Drol setaredefonc evarb ruo sselb dog
drageruaeb dna htims nosnhoj eel
eoj nosnhoj dna htims noskcaj pleh
ho eixid ni stif meht evig ot

The newspaper published the Sanskrit example along with the "beautiful and patriotic poem by our talented contributor." A few days later some sharp reader discovered the trick and exposed it, to the embarrassment of the Boston newspaper. The Sanskrit example was really an English verse spelled backward. With punctuation added, it said:

God bless our brave Confederates, Lord!
Lee, Johnson, Smith, and Beauregard!
Help Jackson, Smith, and Johnson Joe,
To give them fits in Dixie, oh!

General Hoffman was so impressed with what Anna had done that he wrote her complimenting her on her wit and asking that she favor him with early copies of any future poetic productions.

Reference:

Wickham Hoffman, *Camp Court and Siege* (New York: Harper and Brothers, Publishers, 1877).

Jean Lafitte Almost Brought Napoleon to Louisiana

While Jean Lafitte, the legendary pirate, dominated the shipping lanes around Cuba and throughout the Gulf of Mexico, one of his land bases was in southwest Louisiana in an area known as the Neutral Strip. This area, bounded by the Sabine River on the west and the Calcasieu River on the east, had earlier been unofficially set aside by the United States and Spanish governments as an area where neither government would impose its jurisdiction. Thus the so-called Neutral Strip became a haven and a refuge for the lawless and the outcasts of both nations. It therefore became a natural resort for Lafitte and his men between some of their sea excursions.

The pirate Lafitte was also an entrepreneur who stole slaves as well as treasure. Carrying on a lucrative slave trade on Galveston Island and in the Neutral Strip, he sold captured Africans throughout Texas and Louisiana.

While plundering Spanish and English shipping, Lafitte remained a faithful servant to his native France. When things were not going well for the French aristocracy in 1811, Lafitte received a princely sum of money to pick up Charles Sallier and others who had escaped to Spain and bring them to Louisiana. As he sailed with his refugees into Lake Charles, dozens of Atakapa Indians welcomed Lafitte's arrival by scampering into their dugouts and rowing out to meet the ship. Thoroughly frightened at this seemingly hostile action, Sallier dashed below deck to warn Lafitte of the impending danger.

"Calm yourself, my dear sir," Lafitte responded. "They are my friends and will do my slightest bidding."

And indeed, it turned out to be a warm and joyous welcoming that the sailors received.

In 1815 following his disastrous defeat at Waterloo, Napoleon Bonaparte avoided capture and made his way back to

Paris. Knowing that Louis XVIII would soon be returning to reclaim the French throne, Napoleon's aides arranged for Lafitte to come to France and this time transport Napoleon himself to Louisiana. On the appointed night, Lafitte's men loaded a score of sea chests containing Napoleon's personal fortune, but after Napoleon failed to make his own appearance, Lafitte's ship had to sail away without him. Napoleon had tarried too long in Malmaison, and after missing his anticipated rendezvous with Lafitte, he chose to surrender to the English and suffer a second exile (this time to the island of St. Helena off the coast of Africa) rather than submit to the retribution of Louis XVIII.

It was rumored at the time that Lafitte's men carried Napoleon's chests ashore and buried them in some marsh beside the Calcasieu River, but this is a mystery that probably never will be solved. And one can only wonder how American and European history might have been altered had Lafitte been able to bring Napoleon to Louisiana as planned.

Reference:

W. T. Block, "The Legacy of Jean Lafitte," *True West*, November-December 1979.

Index